Servant Leadership

Leading with a Purpose

Dr. Ronnie Melton, D. Min, LPC, CPCS, NCC

Copyright © 2021

All Rights Reserved

ISBN: 978-1-80128-166-9

Dedication

This book is dedicated to my parents George Melton Jr. and Mae Frances Melton. Thanks for your love and support. You said I was going to do it.

Acknowledgements

First and foremost, praises and thanks to my Lord and Savior Jesus Christ for showering me with blessings throughout my work to complete my first book successfully. Thank you, God, for keeping me grounded in the project. The best is yet to come.

I am extremely grateful to my parents George Melton Jr. and Mae Frances Melton for their love, prayers, care, and sacrifices for educating and preparing me for this moment in my life. I am very much thankful to my wife Carol for her love, understanding, prayers, and continuing support to complete this work. Thanks for stretching me and never complaining. As I marched on this journey, you were brave enough to march with me.

I would like to express special thanks to my sister Teresa and brothers George, Dennis, and Steven. I am so grateful to be called your little brother. I would like to thank other family members for their support and valuable prayers. My special thanks to Bishop Leslie Patterson Jr., who opened the door when I received my calling from God and provided me with knowledge and wisdom in the word of God. This is the secret to success. Special thanks to my Goddaughter Aliyah Nickens, who has been such an inspiration over the years. Thanks to my special friend and Cock-a-poo "Jet." Your special and kind personality kept me going when I was tired and ready to quit.

I would like to say thanks to my friends and extended family while I traveled over 20 years in the military. It was those friends who encouraged me to reach for the stars. Finally, my thanks to all the people who supported me in completing the research work directly or indirectly.

About the Author

Dr. Ronnie Melton is a Licensed Ordained Minister for over 22 years. He is also a retired Master Sergeant in the United States Army, where he served for 23 years. During his life's journey, he became a Certified Chaplain and College Adjunct Professor. His education consists of a bachelor's degree in Criminology, a Master's in Christian Counseling, and a second Master's in Mental Health Counseling. He continued his education with a doctoral degree in Ministry and a second doctoral in Human Services (ABD). Dr. Ronnie Melton is also a Licensed Professional Counselor (LPC) and Neuroscience Leader and Coach. Dr. Melton currently has been selected to begin his third doctoral degree in Clinical Pastoral Counseling and Psychology.

Preface

This book is written through the grace of God, for the people of God, so that they may benefit from the wisdom in His infinite knowledge. It is for all the pastors, leaders and aspiring trailblazers who want to find their own way in this world, who seek to inspire for the greater good and who are ready to give it their all in order to help change the unjust prospects of the world. Qualities of leadership are something everyone needs when they are standing on the front lines of any laborious task.

This book encompasses everything there is to know about great leadership, and how one can acquire that trait. From what it means to be a leader to an excellent leader's disposition, this meticulously written text covers a wide array of topics giving you a comprehensive list of tips that will, not only help you in your task of being a pastor or as a superintendent in the corporate world, but would also help you as you journey through life. For even if you don't have a followership to shadow you in your footsteps, you, your heart, body, mind and soul are your eternal companions on this extensive pathway. You need to know how to find your own way when deprived of everything else so that you can reach the destination you want without needing guidance. A mind carrying wisdom can help change the world, and if not, it can surely help change one's own life.

Contents

Page Left Blank Intentionally

Introduction

"Servanthood does not nullify leadership; instead, it defines it. Jesus does not cease to be the lion of Judah when He becomes the lamb-like servant of the church." ***-John Piper***

Throughout our professional lives, we are made to look up to one particular figure of authority. Some of these people are the ones who are there just for the sake of being there. These individuals add minimal value to our lives, and not much would change if they were replaced with someone else. Then there are those who touch us deeply and have so much to offer. We cannot help but fall for these people. We even try to incorporate some of their personality traits into ours.

So, what is the difference between the two categories of people that I have just mentioned? Simple, people hailing from the first category are merely bosses and administrators, while the latter is what we refer to as leaders.

Then there is another category in which only great leaders reside. These are the people who compel you to be the best version of yourself. Because of them, you get to meet yourself truly. They possess a deep understanding of people and know how to communicate with them, regardless of who they are and where they are coming from. Interestingly, these people aren't full of themselves. They understand their flaws well enough. They are always seeking knowledge, and to them, every second of their lives is a learning opportunity. Moreover, these are the people you go to for help, especially when you are shattered and broken.

Contrary to popular belief, these people aren't coming from a place of perfection. In their lives, they have had their fair share of adversity and hardship. Surprisingly, the miseries and sorrows of life do little to bring them down. They make peace with life's difficulties and struggles, only to become much stronger versions of themselves. To understand that suffering is an inevitable part of human existence, they train themselves to keep on maneuvering without breaking down. Challenges don't easily trigger these people, and instead of snapping and taking it out on the people around them, they study the situation they are in and evaluate their options to help them push through.

A major part of my life was spent trying to find the answer to the question, "What makes great leaders great?" As simple as it seems, it took me several years to find the answer. Whether it was my school or workplace, there would always be this specific person I was drawn toward, and secretly somewhere inside, I wanted to be like them. No matter how hard I tried, I ended messing myself up even more, which only added to my confusion, frustration, and angst. However, I realized that instead of adopting their traits, I was just a copycat who was trying too hard to impersonate something I could never have been. I also realized that all of us have a spark, which, if ignited, would enable us to become exemplary leaders without having to impersonate somebody else just because their demeanor appealed to us.

The experience of trying to be something I was not did not only frustrate me but also infuriated me at the same time. Because of the fruitless effort, I grew more and more oblivious of my gift. Something inside me pushed me to become more focused on what and where God was trying to lead me. There I took the road of indulging myself in a variety of bookstores. I had to find out my purpose in life.

It was in Saint Petersburg, FL, where I delved into it, as deep as I possibly could, hoping to find the answer. It was then that I discovered what an exceptional man Jesus was. Not that I was not raised in the Church. I was intrigued by Jesus and took it upon myself as my life's purpose to explore even the tiniest nitty-gritty I could find on him. The more I read up on Him, the more I felt my image of a great leader fading, and finally, I was finding some clarity.

Before I read about Jesus, my idea of leadership was very myopic. Without even knowing it, I connected leadership with self-righteousness, which totally defeats a leader's purpose. It helped me realize that a leader isn't arrogant, and if he is, then he is nothing more than a tyrant, who is used to getting things done by hook or crook. Instead, a leader is humble and compassionate. He is humble before God, and it is his mission to work toward the betterment of God's creation.

A great leader doesn't spend his time trying to convince people to perform in a certain way. Instead, he practices what he preaches, and through his actions and lifestyle, he inspires the people around him to adopt the traits that he possesses. Jesus was the perfect personification of everything you would seek in a great leader.

I have spent a considerable part of my life interacting with successful corporate heads, as well as men of God. In the case of these corporate heads, they have a lot to bring to the table, yet they have a hard time adding to the productivity of those who work under them. No matter how hard they try to inspire their employees, something always falls short. The irony is that even they don't know the answer.

Similarly, the men of God scuffle to convey the divine message to the common man. However, somehow their efforts always go in vain and they also have a hard time finding the answer. This is why I have put together this book. It gives you an insight into what it takes to be a great leader, so I hope you will use it to your advantage.

Chapter 1: The Making of a Leader

Whether it is an organization, a community, or a group of people, leadership plays a crucial role in their well-being. The true purpose of leadership is to influence people's minds and behaviors to strive toward fulfilling a shared cause. A leader should have immaculate interpersonal skills, and at the same time, he should motivate his subordinates to be better at whatever they do.

Significance of a Leader

A true leader is the one who takes the initiative and stands by his decision right till the very end. It wouldn't be incorrect to say that a leader's job is right at the beginning before the real work actually begins. He is the one who conceptualizes a task, evaluates his options, and mobilizes the resources and the workforce required to move toward the completion of a task. Moreover, he is the one who communicates to his people the policies and protocols needed to do a job properly.

Contrary to popular belief, the role of a leader isn't an easy one. Do you want to know why? There are times when your subordinates aren't motivated to perform. That is when the real panic kicks in and the people who are unable to hold their nerves tend to snap. However, a true leader listens to the reservations and the grievances of his subordinates and motivates them. Sometimes, he does it through mere words of motivation, while sometimes there is an incentive attached. He understands the significance of motivation and encouragement and uses the two to get things done efficiently.

Some people believe that a leader only supervises those who work under him. This approach is partially true, but supervising is just a small fraction of all the things a leader does. A leader does supervise, but he also guides his subordinates in whatever they are doing. He always follows up on their work and provides them with timely feedback, which includes valuable tips and suggestions to eliminate their mistakes while doing the task effectively and efficiently. He always makes sure that the efforts of his subordinates do not get wasted.

Another important part of being a leader is to develop confidence in the people who look up to you. Sometimes, people possess the ability and skills needed to execute a particular task. However, it is the lack of experience which results in a low level of confidence. The absence of confidence often makes the best of an individual's lag. However, this is where a leader can be a game-changer. He understands this well enough and does everything he can to make sure his subordinates believe in their ability to perform. To do this, he acknowledges the performance and the efforts of the people under him. He also entertains any complaints and grievances as well as comes up with timely solutions to the problems. As a result, he builds confidence in the people to whom he assigns certain tasks.

Furthermore, a leader creates a suitable environment, which is conducive to creativity and where new ideas are born. He allows his subordinates to provide their input and listens to them with an open mind. There are times when people do not agree with him. He doesn't take anything personally and provides his subordinates with a logical explanation for the steps he takes, which helps him convince his subordinates. Another thing that he is good at is conflict resolution. He listens to everyone with patience before he concludes. The environment that he creates is the one in which everyone is a winner. It results in the organization's progress and growth.

Another thing that a true leader strives to ensure is coordination. In a setting where there are more than two people involved, individual interests often tend to overlap with the interests of the entire group or the company. As a result, conflicts are born and the greater goal is overshadowed with unnecessary things and forgotten halfway through. A leader makes sure that the personal interests of the employees align perfectly with those of the environment.

No matter how competent a leader is, he cannot always stick around to keep an eye on whether everything is going according to plan. In his absence, things can collapse, but somehow they don't. Have you ever thought why things continue to happen smoothly while the leader is away? The answer is simple and straightforward. A true leader is the one who leaves his successors to take charge of everything while he isn't around. A leader handpicks some of the best people in his team and trains them well. These chosen ones can take over, just in case their leader isn't around. As a result, he creates more leaders who can fit into his shoes when the circumstances call for it.

You might be the most competent person on the team. However, it doesn't mean that you will be just as welcoming to new changes. When things shift for the better or for worse, it becomes hard for people to maintain a balance. Accepting changes and adapting to them quickly is easier said than done. Some people often welcome changes with a great amount of disgust. A leader makes sure his teammates and subordinates are always ready to accept changes and take on new challenges without the slightest amount of resistance. As a result, he conditions them so that accepting changes for them becomes the norm.

Traits of a Leader

Up until now, we have talked about the significance of what it means to be a leader. In this part, we will look at some of the many traits that a leader possesses.

One of the traits of a true leader is a pleasing personality. A leader's personality is such that it unintentionally attracts people from a mile away. People are drawn toward such personalities without even realizing it and rarely do they walk away empty-handed. Moreover, a leader isn't completely authoritative but is also friendly at the same time. However, he can assert his dominance where it is due and get things done the way he wants them to be done.

Another trait of a true leader is that he is knowledgeable. In this scenario, the word 'knowledge' has little to do with what you learn in school. Over here, knowledge has more to do with the things that you acquire through experience. Because of his knowledge and a firm grasp over his niche, the subordinates are compelled to reach him for suggestions. Knowledge combined with competence is a killer duo that a leader utilizes to influence the people that he is in charge of.

Besides having an attractive personality and knowledge, a true leader also possesses another worthy trait, which is integrity. He never lets go of his integrity and remains honest and fair throughout the process. He has a positive outlook on most things and never comes up with a judgment unless backed with facts and logic. Furthermore, a leader is never biased. He is always objective with his approach. He doesn't hold any grudges against his people. Instead, he gives credit where it is due open-heartedly.

Moreover, a leader is always on the lookout for opportunities. It doesn't mean that he manipulates and takes advantage of people. It simply means that he always keeps an eye out for things that will eventually help him reach his goal. Whenever an opportunity presents itself, he grabs it with both hands and capitalizes on it to fulfill his goals. As a result, he develops a deep knowledge of what is going on in his surroundings, which helps him deal with scams and all sorts of fraudulent activities.

Another trait of a true leader is that he possesses good communication skills. To be a true leader, you have to be excellent when it comes to communicating. With the right communication skills, he can easily convey his messages and ideas to the people he manages. Part of being a good communicator has a lot to do with being an avid listener. A leader listens to his teammates and subordinates very patiently and examines the situation well before coming up with a suggestion. Hence, only a small percentage of his decisions ever go wrong, for there is a significant amount of thought that goes into those decisions.

It is almost sinful for a leader to act weak in front of his disciples. No matter how troubled or confused he is, he cannot freak out nor break down in front of his subordinates. Instead, a leader possesses unshakable self-confidence and willpower. No matter how exhausting the circumstances are, a true leader always steps up to the challenge and leads his people by example. If he loses his composure during trying times, he won't be a leader, and nor will his followers ever look up to him.

Another thing that you will find common among all leaders is intelligence. Knee-jerk reactions to situations are unknown to a leader. Before he reaches a decision, he thinks multiple times and entertains suggestions. He also analyzes and evaluates his options as well as the pros and cons of the situation that is presented to him. Moreover, he possesses great foresight of the future. Because of his intelligence, he can predict the outcomes of his actions and decisions. Furthermore, he is very decisive toward his actions and decisions and stays firm even if the odds are against him.

Lastly, a true leader possesses great social skills. Despite exercising control, he is always empathetic toward the needs of his followers and the people surrounding him. Unlike a boss, a leader has a humanitarian side to his personality. He also helps people deal with their problems. He considers himself responsible and accountable for the well-being of the people around him. This trait is often rewarded by loyalty.

Components of a Great Leader

By now, you must have understood the significance of being a leader as well as the traits a leader possesses. However, those things are just a fraction of a leader's personality. The components or the building blocks of a great leader's persona are what differentiate between him and an ordinary leader or a follower.

As we have already discussed, a great leader is inspirational and believes in leading by example. It gives him great pleasure to contribute to the well-being of the people around him or the ones who look up to him. He encourages and motivates people to be the best version of themselves. Never does he use force to get the desired results. His words, actions, and even the way he carries himself are enough to make people want to be like him. Enabling people to achieve great things is the greatest pleasure that he can ask for, and he doesn't ask for anything in return. This component of his personality is something that brings him closer to God. They make their followers believe in themselves in a way that there is no hand-holding required.

Another component of a great leader is the ability to understand different types of people. No matter who you are, where you come from, and what you have to offer, a leader will not judge you whatsoever. Instead, he will put in the time and the effort needed to understand your personality, your wants, your likes and dislikes, strengths and weaknesses, and aspirations to be able to help you.

At the same time, he will have great communication skills. When you speak to him, never for a minute will you think you are communicating with a stranger. Instead, you will feel as if you both have known each other for ages. He will listen very carefully to every word that comes out of your mouth and respond to you in a way that you are familiar with. Speaking to him will be just like speaking to God on a bad day. God doesn't turn his people away and nor does a true leader.

Moreover, a true leader is humble. Being full of himself is the last thing that he can be. On the flip side, a boss will be self-obsessed and will do everything in his power to prove that he is right.

A great leader isn't Mr. perfect and feels no shame in admitting his flaws. He also doesn't feel any shame whenever he makes a mistake. He knows that mistakes are the only way forward, and to him, they are his greatest teachers. He isn't careless enough to commit mistakes on purpose but doesn't mind if he makes a few, for they are the ones that cultivate in him the creative nectar needed to do great things. At the same time, he is always reading, researching, and learning new things. He is perfectly in tune with the latest technologies and the latest ideas, for he doesn't want to lag and expects his followers to do the same. He doesn't deny a good thing, even if it is coming from one of his juniors, and acknowledges it with an open heart.

Most conventional managers and supervisors are lazy because they are so used to their old ways that anything new is almost scary to them. On the flip side, a genuine leader looks at life as if it is one big learning opportunity. He doesn't mind unlearning outdated concepts and ideas and having them replaced with new ones. The only thing that matters to him is moving forward and enabling his colleagues and subordinates to follow in his footsteps.

One more component of a true leader that almost gives him a God-like status is that people go up to him in times of need. Whenever you feel shattered and broken, or even if you're having a bad day, there will always be someone you would go to, knowing that they will console you and try to make you feel better while helping you come out of the situation that you are in at the moment. As a person who looks up to him, you somehow feel as if he has the answers to all of your problems, and even if he can't solve your problems, he makes sure that you don't have to face them alone.

Responsibilities of a Leader

If you have ever been in a professional setting, you can understand what happens when poor leadership takes over. One of the most common consequences of poor leadership is a confused workforce and productivity that keeps going down the drain.

Here are some of the most common responsibilities of a leader.

Building Trust

As a leader, you must be able to develop a level of trust with your team members. Interestingly, building trust isn't as simple as it seems to most people. It is like a three-way pattern, which is broken down in the following points.

- As a leader, you should trust your subordinates.
- Similarly, they should be able to trust you.

- They should also trust each other.

Trust doesn't come overnight, so you have to work your way toward it. To build trust, you should initiate short team-building activities where people can interact with one another for some time. Moreover, refrain from assigning tasks that are beyond your team's skillset. Such a mistake can harm the relationship that you try to build with your team.

Offering Significant Autonomy and Resources

A team of people often fails when they run short of time and resources needed to do a job. As a leader, you should be aware of the capabilities of your team members. This will allow you to determine the time and resources you need to provide them to get a job done efficiently.

Moreover, it would be impossible for you to stick around and keep an eye on whatever is going on. Therefore, it is better to appoint a team lead who looks after things while you are away. The team lead or captain should make sure your protocols and procedures are followed properly in your absence. Furthermore, you shouldn't micromanage the team, or else they will start to feel a little suffocated. Instead, it is better to allow them some autonomy to complete the assigned tasks freely.

Cultivating Team Efficacy

There are some tasks in which the team members do not feel confident enough to perform. That is where your role as a leader comes in. You should appreciate and acknowledge their efforts and boost their confidence, so they can believe in their abilities to handle challenging tasks. If one of your team members doesn't feel up for the task, try pairing him up with a high-achiever. This will motivate him to believe in himself, thus he will perform better.

Ask your team members to be vocal about their fears and insecurities. As a result, not only will they trust you, but there will come a time when they will find their insecurities disappearing.

Ensuring Accountability

No matter how experienced or skilled your team members are, they should always be held accountable for their actions and the decisions they make. This doesn't mean you have to torture them psychologically. Instead, this will end up working in favor of the employee and the entire team.

Chapter 2: Vision Is the Key

"Where there is no vision, the people perish, but he that keepeth the law, happy is he." ***-Proverbs 29:18***

In the world that we live in, there is a majority of people who spend their entire lives searching for purpose. To the world, they are normal, living, and breathing creatures, but inside them resides a lot of disturbance. They spend their time deeply dissatisfied with their potential. They question their ability at every step and seek validation from those around them. This self-doubt and the need for approval from others keep such people from performing optimally. They find it difficult to achieve their goals. The only problem with these people is that they lack vision; hence, their efforts are fruitless, and rarely do they reap the fruit of their input.

When it comes to leadership, there are a host of things needed to succeed as a leader. You might have a great physique backed by a mesmerizing persona, but some serious work needs to be done if the vision is missing. In the absence of vision, you cannot convince a group of people to follow you toward achieving a common goal. If you are lucky, you might convince a few confused souls who are used to holding hands, but your mission won't see the light of day and won't materialize.

It wouldn't be wrong to say that a leader without a vision should be classified as just another individual, except an individual who doesn't have a head on his shoulders. A visionless leader is just a mere wanderer, or worse, a pendulum who just hangs there. One of the perfect examples of leadership vision was the one that was possessed by Moses. In the name of God, the man inspired an entire nation to do the things that they couldn't have even imagined themselves doing. His vision as a leader was backed by surrender to God, humanity to man, and a sheer amount of compassion. Raised as the prince of Egypt, he made the people realize how oppressed they were. By doing so, he ignited in them a spark for freedom and it got to the point that they followed him right in the middle of the sea, when everywhere they looked, there was instant death. He made his people understand that freedom was their birthright and that they should fight injustice, oppression, and tyranny wherever they saw it.

So, what exactly is a vision? Well, there is a conclusive answer to this question. Throughout history, the vision has been defined differently by different people, depending upon what they had in mind. For an average person without any significant aspiration, a vision is nothing but a dream. The only problem is that we make new dreams every day only to have them replaced with new ones. Interestingly, we grow more and more uninterested in the things that we fail to accomplish, and then those dreams find their way into the secret archives of our mind, never to be unlocked again. The people in this category might have an exciting dream one day and an entirely different dream the next day. These people spend a considerable amount of time jumping from one place to another, whether it is their work, academics, or even interpersonal relationships. A person who is so indecisive and inconsistent with his dreams can never become a leader unless he mends his ways. Not only do these people find it hard to achieve great things, but the worst part is that they aren't even happy with their lives. Some of them even go the extra mile and fall prey to anxiety and depression issues.

Up until now, we have spoken about the meaning of vision for an average human being. However, the meaning of vision for a leader is a totally different story. For a leader, a vision is not only a dream that he forgets the next day. Instead, a leader's vision is a set of long-term goals, which are further broken down into several short-term goals that he has to achieve to work his way toward having what he wants to have. In the process of achieving his goals, he streamlines his alternatives, calculates the risks involved, and evaluates the efficacy of every one of his options before he sets things in motion. He believes utterly in the beauty of his dreams and doesn't mind being adventurous. His ways involve a lot of trial and error, of which failure is a crucial component. However, initial setbacks do little to break him down. He continues to move forth and doesn't scale down on his ambitions.

There is another aspect of a leader's vision. A true leader doesn't pursue a dream until it resonates with his moral values and belief systems. First of all, he won't go after a dream that collides with the things he believes in. Secondly, he will make sure the means of achieving his goal are fair without the slightest amount of fraud. With such an approach, a leader finds it easy to inspire and convince others to follow him. His teammates and subordinates respect the fact that he doesn't compromise on his values and beliefs. Therefore, they stick with him, even if his initial attempts at fulfilling a specific goal result in failure.

Furthermore, a leader doesn't go for his goal in haste. Instead, he is patient and allows himself the time it takes to do the job well. During this time, he examines the playing field and adapts to the situation before he makes a move. Therefore, the chances of failure are scarce, and even in the case of failure, he understands where he went wrong so that he can troubleshoot his mistakes going forth.

Then there is a category of people, who have a vision in life, but somehow they find it hard or even impossible to go about it. Some of them don't pursue their vision, while some of them don't even acknowledge it. The only thing that holds them back is the fact that their vision seems too far-fetched or unattainable. Instead of going after the things that fire them up, these people are often seen inspiring others to follow their hearts and live their dreams. They are either too scared or too busy or distracted to materialize their vision.

As we have discussed earlier, the people who have no vision are often unable to perform. Therefore, they are often found frustrated with their lives. They have a lot of angry outbursts, and for them, their bitter behavior is a way of getting back at the world. They fail to realize that their anger and frustration only make them feel more miserable, without doing much good. Instead of making a list of goals and comparing them with the list of options at hand, these people are extreme in coming up with excuses for their failure

There are several reasons why a person needs a vision in his life. Without it, you will get stuck at each step. The worst part is that you won't even realize why. It is the vision that helps you get up in the morning. It is what motivates you to step out in pursuit of your goal.

It also affects the level of effectiveness with which you execute a particular task. It also helps you identify the mistake, just in case you go wrong somewhere. It adds purpose to your life and allows you to communicate your ideas to the people you look up to. Furthermore, it is the vision that keeps you attached to your morals and belief system. It also prevents you from deviating from your path.

People who lack vision are often seen complaining about the cruelties of life and how the forces outside their control keep them from pursuing what they want. When it comes to interpersonal relationships, they fail to take the initiative and take the lead so that others can benefit. Instead, they come up with the excuse that others don't cooperate with them in a way that is expected by them. Similarly, when such people are in an organizational setting, they blame their failure because of the lack of resources or a good team of people. If only they had the vision, none of that would have happened. Instead, it would have been the other way around.

A leader who has a vision is happy and satisfied with himself, his life, as well as the world that surrounds him. Furthermore, he accepts the situation for how it is, and despite the adversities, he stays hopeful. The best thing about visionary leaders is the fact that he does not fear change. Instead, he views change as a means to move forward. He makes full use of his strengths. At the same time, he isn't oblivious to his weaknesses. He puts in enough effort to eliminate his shortcomings, but he doesn't spend a single minute stressing them. Similarly, he does not fear failure, and the best thing for him is a mistake. For him, the mistake is the greatest teacher to a visionary leader. He views mistakes as breakthroughs that open the doors to new possibilities rather than obstructions. He is persistent and understands that he will eventually meet his target if he keeps on going.

Creating a Leadership Vision

Contrary to popular belief, nobody is born with a leadership vision. Instead, such a vision is cultivated with time. Such a vision comes into existence when you are met with challenging situations where you don't have the option to shy away or back off. Leadership vision doesn't come overnight. It takes some time before you can train your mind to think in a certain manner. To develop that kind of vision, a person needs to conduct a thorough assessment of the self, keeping the environment in view. A vision is something that is entirely intangible, but you have to hold on to it for you to be able to achieve great things. One of the most common questions asked revolves around how to develop the perfect leadership vision.

In the following paragraphs, we will discuss a step-by-step breakdown of what it takes to cultivate a leadership vision.

- The first and foremost step on the road to developing a leadership vision is to know and accept yourself the way you are. You should value your individuality for you are unique, instead of wasting your time trying to be a socially acceptable version. Similarly, you should be fully aware of your strengths and weaknesses. You should act intelligent enough to benefit from your strengths while trying to eliminate your shortcomings.

- Secondly, you should be well aware of your moral values and belief system. Before you take a step, you must measure your move with the things that you believe in. If they align perfectly, there is nothing that can stop you from moving forward. However, if they don't align, you should continue the search for your options.

- The goals that you set should be realistic yet challenging. A goal that isn't challenging isn't a goal. It is just a dream that gets forgotten like many other dreams that we see every night. If your goals don't challenge you, they won't change you, and hence, you won't be able to become the visionary leader that you set out to become. Also, you should set some priorities, and your performance should be measured at each step. Measuring your performance lets you understand how close you are to achieving your goal.

- The goal descriptions that you have should be simple, short, and straightforward. They shouldn't be convoluted by unnecessary things, for they only confuse you and drive you far away from developing a vision. The goal description should also align perfectly with your values, ethics, and morals.

- Furthermore, your dreams should be unique. You should go after the things that excite you, instead of what others have or enjoy doing. Your dreams and aspirations should be such that they challenge the status quo. Your goals should be different in a way that they inspire others to step out of the box and think big.

- Your dreams shouldn't remain stagnant over a period of time. Instead, you can expand your dream or combine your existing dreams with newer and bigger ones. It will help if you revisit your dreams from time to time, keeping in mind the environment and the situation around you. This will allow you the time you need to tweak your strategy just a little. Sometimes, the modifications that you make to your strategy play a crucial role in helping you maneuver through difficult times.

Sustaining the Leadership Vision

Being able to come up with a leadership vision seems difficult, but it is fairly simple in reality. The real challenge is being able to sustain that vision and holding on to it. Once you have the vision in place, you need to make a few things to make it more vivid and simple. The following points will help you on the way.

- As we have already mentioned in the previous paragraphs, one of the best ways to sustain your leadership vision is to revisit your vision from time to time. You need to make sure it is up to date and perfectly in tune with the changing environment, which becomes more and more competitive with each passing minute. By revisiting your vision, you develop interesting new ways to strengthen your vision as time passes.

- If you are in charge of an entire establishment or even a group of people, you will have to lead from the front. You can only do this when your vision resonates perfectly with the vision of the people who look up to you. Therefore, you need to come up with a vision statement. It should be perfectly in sync with your morals and values.

- This is the most difficult one, and it is easier said than done. The vision that you have come up with can only be sustained when it is well-grounded into your organization's culture or the people you are in charge of. Moreover, it should reflect through your employees, products, and the services that you provide. Most importantly, the vision should be embedded in your business' core values, which is reflected through your employees' behavior.

- Never make promises and commitments if you can't follow them through right till the very end. Always make sure you keep your promises. By doing so, you hold yourself accountable, which in turn makes you more responsible and in a better position to sustain your vision effectively and convey it to the people who look up to you. Also, the tasks you perform should be executed with your utmost diligence. You might be the head of a department or even the entire organization but never treat a task as if it is negligible and far below your job description.

- As a leader with vision, it is extremely important to be an expert at what you are trying to make others do for you. If you don't, you can never lead by example. Your subordinates will never take you seriously, nor will they have a fear of being held accountable for their actions. They will know that no matter what they do, they will get away with it without any questions asked. But what's more important is that you have a solid character along with workplace expertise. Even if you fall short of skills, you will stand by your team through thick and thin, and they will stand by you when the time comes.

- Whether you are a good boss or not, your team will eventually look up to you. When a couple of people get together to achieve a goal, there are times when things don't go according to plan, and sometimes things go a little sideways. Such situations can be scary, but for a leader who holds onto his vision and imparts it to others, they aren't all that intimidating. As a visionary leader, you stay optimistic and maintain a positive outlook. As a result, your teammates and subordinates will stay strong throughout the trying times, thus becoming better individuals, and the credit will be yours.

- One of the best ways to sustain your vision is to communicate it to your subordinates through storytelling. It needs a certain level of creativity, but it is the real deal and one that always helps. Using your storytelling skills, you must teach your employees loyalty, sincerity, and commitment. You should also try your best to keep them motivated, just in case one feels as if they are burning out, which happens a lot in today's extremely competitive work environment. It would help if you also challenged them to do better at their job. Never make the horrendous mistake of forcing your vision onto your employees. Instead, use your well-crafted stories to inspire them in a way that they adopt the vision that you want them to have.

- Cultivating a vision and holding on to your vision is difficult. There will be times when you run into people who don't necessarily agree with your vision. These are the people we refer to as naysayers. These people will find flaws in your vision on purpose and criticize it, even if they agree with what you have to offer. Your job is to listen to their criticism with a lot of patience and not compromise your vision by losing temper and snapping completely. There is another situation in which you would succumb to the pressure they exert and you might want to agree with them. Remember, when you meet people who criticize your vision, you must stay calm and hold on to your vision even tighter.

Suppose you are a leader who wants to sustain his vision and wants to impart it to his subordinates. In that case, you should encourage them in every way possible. You should make your subordinates dream big to achieve organizational as well as personal objectives. This way, they will look up to you as their father figure, thus following your vision in whatever they do or the situation they find themselves in.

Vision and Mission Statements

By the subheading above, you must have come to know what we are about to discuss. The term "Vision and Mission Statements" is spoken of more than often in training sessions and the classrooms at business schools. Often, the two concepts are mistaken for one another. In the upcoming paragraphs, we will try to break down the difference between vision and mission statements and take a look at the steps to come up with vision and mission statements of our own, so let's break it down.

A vision statement is the desired position of an organization in the future. On the flip side, a mission statement talks about how certain goals can be achieved. This is part of the reason why the two terms are used interchangeably. Therefore, it is very important to have them both sorted. Interestingly, they both are interdependent on one another. Let's discuss the two concepts in detail.

A *vision statement* gives an organization direction. It revolves around what you want your organization to achieve, and therefore it is aspirational. The vision statement talks about the following.

- Your hopes and dreams

- The problems that need to be solved for a greater benefit
- The things that we want to change

The vision statement is instrumental to both internal and external growth. With a stronger vision, you can develop better teams, which can focus on achieving the things that are good for the organization. It also inspires people within the organization to be more creative and innovative. On the contrary, the lack of vision can be disastrous for an organization and can wreak havoc if left to stay.

A *mission statement* drives companies in the direction they want to head. It gives birth to objectives and the things you need to do to achieve your objectives. A mission statement has a profound impact on a company's culture. Here are a few simple questions the mission statement seeks to answer.

- What are we going to do?
- Who are we going to serve?
- How are we going to serve them?

Now that we have discussed both vision and mission statements, let's shift gears and talk about how vision and mission statements are written.

The following simple steps will help you come up with an effective mission statement.

- The first thing that you need to do when crafting a mission statement is to define your purpose. You need to ask yourself about the reason behind the existence of your organization. Try coming up with a list of the products and the services that you provide.

Then come up with another list that talks about your targeted groups. By doing so, you will find yourself in a better position to communicate your purpose and ideas to your potential customers and team members.

- Next up, if you want to craft an effective mission statement, make sure it is specific and to the point. The last thing that you would want to do to your mission statement is to stuff it with jargon and filler words. For example, in your mission statement, you can say, "We provide brands with unparalleled media planning services." This statement can sink in easily, for it is simple and straightforward. On the flip side, if you come up with something like, "We offer research-backed ad placement strategies which provide an amazing return on investment in real time," your targeted audience will have a hard time understanding what you want to convey. Before you know it, they will bounce. The latter statement is wordy and contains industry-specific terminologies that a layman might have a hard time coming to terms with. It will also be difficult for your team members to remember such phrases. Also, be very particular about the length of your statements, as well as the choice of words.

- It is a fact that your mission statement should be simple and understandable. However, it is just as important to keep it inspirational. It should be able to galvanize your team members and motivate them to perform well. Furthermore, it is very important to have your mission statement tied to a particular set of activities and behaviors. By doing so, you can allow yourself and your team members to transition from being very bookish to more practical.

- A lot of the companies out there keep their mission statements extremely wordy, which, in a way, is fine. It is elaborate and provides the readers with an elaborate picture of what the organization does. However, it is not the best thing to do when conveying your organization's message. Make sure your mission statement is as brief and concise as possible. However, if you choose to keep it big and wordy, try to keep your delivery very sharp and catchy.

Now that we are through the step-by-step process to craft a mission statement, let's talk about the vision statement. In the following paragraphs, you will learn how to come up with a vision statement. So, let's break it down.

- First of all, make sure your entire team is on board. Now that everyone is under one roof, ask all of them to make their suggestions regarding what the vision statement should be. It should be precise and must resonate with the purpose of your business.

- The vision statement should be short and simple, and it should be memorable. It must motivate you and your team members to move in the direction you want your organization to move.

- One of the most important components of a good vision statement is inclusivity. All the people in your team should have a feeling of ownership. A vision should be achieved through mutual consensus rather than imposed on people by some supreme authority.

- The vision statement is more of a promise rather than a mere statement. You must never make promises that you cannot keep. Therefore, the things which are included in your vision statement should be achievable. At the same time, those things should also make your organization evolve and grow.

- After the vision statement is made, it should be made prominent. You can have it printed and pasted on the workstations. It can also be hung from the ceilings in the form of signage, especially in hallways.

- With each passing year, your goals and objectives change. However, every time you develop a new goal, it is better to revisit your vision statement. By doing so, you will realize whether or not you are on the right track. It will also allow you the time you need to troubleshoot your mistakes.

Chapter 3: Influence

Then I said to them, "You see the trouble we are in: Jerusalem lies in ruins, and its gates have been burned with fire. Come, let us rebuild the wall of Jerusalem, and we will no longer be in disgrace." ***Nehemiah (Chapter 2:17)***

At some point in time, we all come across people who have very little to say. But everything that comes out of their mouths is pure gold and has a profound impact on others, as well as the things in their surroundings. These people spend little time explaining themselves and more time taking responsibility and acting upon what they preach. They also inspire people to be the best at whatever they try to accomplish. These people practice more and preach less, which makes them fall into the category of influential leaders.

In the following paragraphs, we will look at some of the aspects of influence that are instrumental in becoming a leader.

- If you aspire to be a charismatic leader, you need to be influential. For influential leaders, one of the biggest aspects of influence is positional power. Such power comes with your rank or the post that you hold within an organizational setup. For example, you head a particular department within a company. In that case, it becomes fairly simple for you to exercise control over most things that happen within your department's umbrella. You can use your influence to address the areas of your choice. Therefore, it becomes easier for you to play your part not only in the decision-making but also in the success of the failure of your organization.

- Emotion is also a very crucial tool when it comes to becoming an influential leader. There are times when you aren't gifted with positional power, yet you want your opinion to be heard for the greater good. However, convincing the ones above you to hear you out and act upon what you have to offer isn't the easiest thing. But if you can emotionally influence the ones below you, you enable yourself to turn things in your favor, thus playing your part in achieving a goal. Interestingly, an emotional move will benefit you and those around you, and your superiors will rarely hold it against you.

- Another important aspect of influence is passion. Suppose you aren't passionate about your ideas and convictions. In that case, it is most likely that you will make half-hearted attempts at whatever you are trying to accomplish. Hence, it will become difficult for you to convince those around you to believe in you as well as your ability to do a particular job. Not only should you be passionate, but you must also believe utterly in whatever you do.

- The last and final aspect of influence for leaders is being able to master the art of human interaction. This is easier said than done, for all of us aren't born extroverts. But the good news is that it is not impossible to learn to interact with other individuals and influence them. We human beings are social animals. By putting ourselves in social situations, we can actually learn a lot about other people.

Now, let's shift gears and talk about the traits of an influential leader.

Patience

Because of the movies and the web series we watch every day, the image of an influential leader that we have formed in our heads is extremely flawed and far from reality. First of all, the image of an Alpha and dominant personality that is sold to us is very different than what it should really be. One of the worst notions about an influential leader is that he is a stubborn and brooding man who feeds his ego in every way possible and lashes out in anger if he fails to achieve what he wants. If only we could sit back, relax, and think about it with an open mind, we will conclude that a truly influential leader is the one who is patient. He controls his impulses and exercises great command over his emotions. He listens to others and pays great attention to what they have to say. He doesn't let his anger get the best of him. It allows him to cultivate healthy relationships with those around him. It is very easy to lead if you are gifted with a set of perfect individuals. The only problem is that no one is perfect, and people always make mistakes. However, if you are patient, you will always find a way to forgive them and teach them not to commit the same mistake over and over again.

Humility

Another trait that is common among all influential leaders is humility. A true leader is down to earth and isn't full of himself. Arrogance and pride can help you get things done in the short run. However, they keep you from going the distance and fail in most cases. Furthermore, the more arrogant and self-righteous you are, the higher the likelihood you will become a pathetic leader. Before you know it, you will be toppled. Also, an arrogant individual is insecure, and insecurity completely defeats the purpose of leadership. It is a fact that as human beings, the need for significance and achievement is too great. However, suppose these needs aren't managed properly. In that case, they can result in unnecessary self-entitlement in a person, which affects the people who surround them. Moreover, to mask his insecurities, a leader will exhibit behavior changes, which are problematic for their subordinates. On the flip side, if you are a humble leader, your subordinates will respect you much more than you expect and will stand by you in your decisions.

Kindness

If you aspire to be an influential leader, you need to ask yourself one simple question, "Am I kind to the people who look up to me?" Ask yourself if you communicate and interact with them in a kind manner or interact with them at all. Do you regret talking to your subordinates or teammates in a tone that you think was questionable or said something harsh? Sometimes, it's not about the tone, but the words are too harsh for someone to bear. Sometimes, there are a few things that are better left unsaid. The only problem is that you need to be kind enough to understand this. A kind leader doesn't mind doing small things for or on behalf of his team members. The best part about kindness is that a kind leader doesn't expect much in return.

Selflessness

Another quality possessed by influential leaders is that they are extremely selfless. They don't have any problem training and mentoring their juniors, making them feel better when their subordinates learn what they want them to learn. On the flip side, a selfish leader expects his subordinates to report to him. He keeps most of the knowledge and information to himself. It makes him feel superior to those he considers below him. He fails to realize that he is doing an utter disservice to no one except himself by doing so. Social media has dominated the world that we live in through and through. Real interactions are becoming more and more uncommon, which is a very dangerous trend. In times like these, it has become fairly easier for every one of us to become self-absorbed in a very major way. To be selfless, you need to be a person of great character. The cases of selfish leadership are around us in all shapes and sizes. Such people only approach their subordinates and team members when they need something or when there is an urgent task that needs completion. That is sheer manipulation. A true leader never manipulates the people who put their trust in him.

Respect

One of the most crucial components of influential leadership is respecting others no matter who they are, where they come from, and what their position is at the present moment. A true leader is the one who does not only present his opinions but also welcomes the opinions of others and even acts upon them if he finds them worthwhile. Furthermore, an influential leader allows others the time they need to talk while he listens patiently with an open mind. Another word for respect is honor. Many of us are extremely sensitive when it comes to honoring. However, some go the extra mile and compromise other people's honor to protect their own. This is where they are ridiculously mistaken. Some people tend to put their subordinates down, hoping that it will help them get more respect, but this is not the case. Suppose you are on the lookout for ways to become an influential leader. In that case, you might try respecting those who look up to you as well as their opinions. You'll be amazed at the amount of respect that you get in return.

Commitment

To become an influential leader, you need character, but the character isn't the only prerequisite needed while you are on the road to becoming a leader of influence. One thing that is just as important as the character is commitment. As a leader, you should be committed to yourself, your goal, and the individuals you aspire to lead. Contrary to popular belief, commitment to yourself doesn't equate to selfishness. In fact, being committed to yourself is a virtue that is crucially important when it comes to becoming a leader of influence. A person who isn't committed to himself will have a hard time believing in his dreams' beauty. He will doubt every move that he makes. Therefore, leading a group of individuals will become impossible. Being committed to your goal and your followers doesn't mean that you become a workaholic or start snooping around your subordinates 24/7. It simply means that you develop a deep understanding of what you want to achieve. You should know the nitty-gritty of how a task needs to be done. Then you must impart that knowledge and skillset to your subordinates and assign certain duties. After the initial stage is done and dusted, your job is to follow it through right till the very end. In the end, you should conduct an evaluation, which will help you eliminate the mistakes and shortcomings, if any. The more committed you are, the higher is the likelihood that you will succeed as a leader.

Honesty

One of the most important traits that people seek in a leader is honesty. Your subordinates and your teammates should know that their best interest is your number one priority. One of the most dangerous trends in our corporate setup, which has been around for quite some time, is that the managers and executives at the top do not necessarily pass down the vision and the direction downward in the organizational hierarchy. Therefore, the people at the bottom are always oblivious to the changes thrown their way. Managers with such an approach keep their subordinates in the dark and their dishonest ways pave the way for sheer distrust between them and their subordinates. Another word for honesty is integrity. This is why these words are often used interchangeably. You might be the most influential and the most powerful person on this planet, but if you lack honesty, you need to do a great amount of thinking. The things that determine your level of honesty are what you do when no one is looking. If you aspire to become an influential person, you need to be a God-fearing person first. Even if you are alone and there is no one watching over you, you should be more than 100% convinced that God is watching you and will hold you accountable for your actions.

Forgiveness

One of the greatest obstacles to progress is our unforgiving attitude toward others, and more dangerously, ourselves. Not only does it keep us from succeeding, but it also pulls us far and far away from God. We make numerous mistakes throughout our lives. Some of them are so bizarre that it seems impossible that they'll ever be forgiven. However, God forgives even the biggest mistakes when we repent from the depth of our hearts. The feelings of unforgiveness continue to eat us from within like a vicious disease, and before we know it, it has already done a considerable amount of damage. The lack of forgiveness can put us under a significant amount of stress and anxiety, resulting in several mental health issues. We should make peace with that all the people around us and we aren't perfect and that is the only thing that makes us human. Otherwise, we'd be nothing more than robots that perform what is expected of them. It is perfectly alright to feel a little angry and frustrated at times. We need to understand that an unforgiving attitude shuts all the doors of opportunity and brings us to a pit-stop that isn't always the prettiest of things. Furthermore, by forgiving those around us or the ones who look up to us, we are actually doing ourselves a favor.

Encouragement and Inspiration

Do you know the difference between a boss and a leader of influence? A boss overpowers his subordinates. His attitude is ridiculous toward the people who look up to him. Such an attitude can be disastrous for the person as well as the organization. On the flip side, an influential leader encourages his teammates and subordinates and motivates them to do better. Interestingly, this motivation is rarely verbal. The true leader never wastes his time talking. Instead, he practices the things that he wants his subordinates to do, and thus he leads by example. He loves to see his followers nurture and helps them grow in whatever way possible.

A Person of Faith

An influential leader possesses several traits that get him closer to God. One such trait is forgiveness. But what is it that cultivates forgiveness in his heart? The answer is simple and straightforward. A true leader understands that God must judge people and hold them accountable for their actions. Therefore, he prefers to forgive and leave things to God. Moreover, he doesn't spend his time stressing the most trivial things. His firm belief is that God loves him greatly and will not abandon him in the toughest of times.

Love for Others

A true leader is pure at heart. He rarely sees the bad in people, which is another thing that brings him closer to God. He understands that people are inherently good, but the system corrupts them and turns them into terribly ugly. He sees the good in everyone, which gives him enough reasons to love people for who they are. He doesn't even expect them to transform themselves into something that he finds acceptable.

Similarly, he believes in the people who he leads and their ability to get a job done the right way. He imparts everything he knows to his followers. He doesn't micro-evaluate their every move, for he believes that people can pick things quickly and possess the ability to put their learning into action in an effective manner. After all, his people's belief results in a lot of trust between him and those who follow him.

Character Not Charisma

We are the unlucky generation of individuals who fall for what is visible to the naked eye and believe it as the truth. Therefore, we spend the least amount of time trying to figure out what truly lies beneath the smooth and shimmery coating of the things we desire, as well as the people we look up to. The content that we consume every day on TV and the internet makes us follow an image of people that is very pleasing to our eyes. Most of us don't even bother to understand the true character of the people who inspire us.

Similarly, a fair majority among us spend a significant portion of our time and money trying to season our outer self. It gets to the point that we don't even care about our character. It is perfectly alright to long for a charismatic persona, but if that persona isn't backed by the character, it is utterly futile. Moreover, without a reasonable character, you will have a hard time influencing people, and even if you manage to do so, it won't last for a very long time.

Leadership is a form of a chain that starts when a person is able to cultivate relationships, and for relationships, the character is needed. In the absence of character, you won't have any relationships, and without relationships, your dream of becoming an influential leader will never see the light of day. So, have you ever asked why the character is of such significant importance? If you have, consider yourself lucky, for in the upcoming paragraphs, all your questions will be answered.

Character Makes You Stand Out

There was a time when people who had charisma would stand way out of the crowd. But, those times are gone, and that doesn't happen very frequently. Maybe with the passage of time, people have become a lot smarter. Nowadays, people who possess charisma manage to stand out, but it is very short-lived. Some of the most common examples of such people are actors, musicians, sportsmen, and corporate tycoons. However, people who possess character are admired by others, and this liking lasts a lifetime.

Character Makes You an Authentic Leader

It wouldn't be wrong to say that becoming a boss is easier than becoming an authentic and influential leader. To emerge as a true leader, you need to possess a set of virtues that not everyone possesses. These include, in particular, honesty, transparency, and the ability to showcase one's beliefs and convictions. These characteristics tend to stay with you for as long as you live and go a long way in shaping your future. Furthermore, charisma is nothing but a glitter that fades away with time. What it leaves behind is something utterly disgusting.

Character Helps Build Trust

So, you want to lead people, and you want them to look up to you as their leader. Have you ever asked yourself why they should do so? Do you know what it is that makes people admire and respect you for who you are? The one thing that will send you through in this quest is trust. If you pluck out trust from the equation, you will lose your right to become a leader. The people who follow you should put their trust in you, and for that to happen, you need to possess a strong character.

Character Makes You Stronger

On numerous occasions, a leader finds himself in situations that are intimidating enough to make them want to quit what they set out to do. However, being in a position of power, it isn't appropriate for them to quit and run away. There will be times when you feel like falling to the ground and succumbing to the pressure that is exerted on you. However, if you possess a strong and exemplary character, you will hold your ground even in the darkest of times. If you cling too much to your charisma, let it be known that your charisma will ditch you when you need it the most. However, it is the strength of your character that provides you with the strength to carry on.

Character Gives Birth to Excellence

It is a no-brainer that if you are a person of character, you'll be able to lead people in a very effective manner. And it doesn't stop there. With a strong character, you will set a good standard for people to follow. The people who look up to you will try to incorporate your personality traits into their own personalities. They will try to become more and more like you. On the flip side, if you lack character, you will lie, cheat, steal, and take shortcuts, and before you know it, your followers will be doing the same. The worst part is that you won't find yourself in a position to stop them. As the old saying goes, *monkey see, monkey do*.

Character Extends Influence

It is a fact that charisma doesn't last long, and after some time, it starts fading away. This is one of the reasons why all the famous celebrities touch their peak only to toil at obscurity for the rest of their days. Charisma is like the gunpowder that is packed inside a firecracker and even creates a loud booming noise followed by a bright spark. But after that, it gets extinguished, never to be fired again. Only the smoke remains, which too rises and becomes part of the atmosphere and then disappears. On the flip side, the character is like a beacon flame that lasts for quite a while, and in some cases, an entire lifetime. It provides light and warmth and continues to burn as long as it receives the fuel. In the case of character, the only types of fuel necessary are kindness, love, compassion, honesty, intelligence, and courage.

Having said that, in the world that we live in, charisma is a crucial tool that helps you make people more aware of your character. You don't have to rely on charisma, but you can utilize it to reach your followers in an effective manner.

However, in the absence of character, it becomes almost impossible to lead a group of people. You constantly have to perform to prove your worth to the people who look up to you. Moreover, with a staunch character, your leadership will strengthen as time passes by. This happens for a reason. With the passage of time, you tend to develop a strong and unbreakable relationship with your followers and teammates. Therefore, the trust you share with them becomes stronger. When that happens, they start putting their faith blindly in you, and even if you fail or commit a mistake, they stand by you and assist you in coming up with the solution to the problem.

The best thing about the character is that it does not only cultivate the qualities of leadership in a person, but it also draws him closer to his maker. Being a leader and a God-fearing individual in today's world isn't something that comes easily. A God-fearing leader is empathetic and isn't oblivious to the problems of his people. He understands very well when his people need some time off and doesn't force them to perform when they feel like doing so.

Chapter 4: Leader's Disposition

One of the saddest things about our generation is the myopic view we have of leadership. A fair majority among us attribute good looks to leadership. Looks play a crucial role in enabling you to influence a group of people, but looks aren't the only thing that you need. To become a great leader, there is a lot more that needs to be done rather than creating a look that is appealing to the eyes of the people.

Some people associate leadership with a thought process, which is fine to an extent. However, leadership is more of instinctive behavior. Behavior is a combination of our overall actions, but at the heart of it all is our attitude. One of the many things that mold an individual leader into an influential and inspiring leader is a positive mental attitude. People with a positive attitude tend to carry themselves like sheer champions. Moreover, their attitude is evident through not only their looks but also their words, as well as their body language. The demeanor of an individual affects the people around them, and therefore, they automatically stand out. People have no issue in accepting them as their leader and want them to take the lead. These people are usually easy to work under. On the flip side, a leader with a negative attitude is often referred to as sad, depressed, and quite difficult to work with.

It doesn't seem like a big deal, but a negative attitude on the part of a leader can be fatal to the work environment. The person may think that their negative attitude is limited to their own self, but it doesn't happen that way. Instead, the vibes they give off give birth to a toxic workplace where inefficiency, laziness, and bullying are the norm. Furthermore, a leader's negative attitude can take its toll on the productivity and the effectiveness of the entire team. If you want people to follow you in a way that has a positive effect on their quality of work, you need to maintain an optimistic attitude.

So, what else do you think a great leader does? A great and influential leader uses his attitude to evoke positive feelings among his subordinates and teammates. He encourages them and motivates them to work their way toward the fulfillment of their goals. His attitude also enables him to listen to the problems and the grievances of his subordinates with an open mind and an even bigger heart and assists him in solving those problems. He understands very well that he cannot solve those problems by himself, but he makes sure his people don't have to face those issues alone.

Contrary to popular belief, to be a leader, you don't have to be the smartest of people. However, to become a leader, you need to have a present mind, so you can lead your team toward the fulfillment of goals and the elimination of problems.

In the case of workplaces, one of the most pivotal things is personality. It is on the basis of personality that conflicts are born, which can make things very messy. A leader understands the personality traits possessed by his team members. One of the things that make him an exemplary leader is the fact that he extracts the best from his team members and utilizes it for the fulfillment of a common goal while working on the traits which aren't so good.

With time, the conventional workplace has transformed into something extremely quick and flexible. A leader with a positive mental attitude understands the importance of adapting to changes. He doesn't spend a single second stressing the changes. He discovers an opportunity in it.

Every leader has a different leadership style, but the one thing that is common among all these leadership styles is a positive mental attitude. Before we move forward, let's spare a moment to take a look at all of these leadership styles.

First on our list is the visionary leader. A visionary leader has a goal in mind. He inspires others to follow him in his direction. He is knowledgeable and creative. At the same time, he is enthusiastic about his work. He inspires his followers through creative ideas and encourages them to come up with things that are unique and non-mainstream.

Then, we have an empathetic leader. He isn't as energetic and innovative as the visionary leader, but the traits that he possesses are far more effective in certain cases. For example, he has a knack for connecting with individuals on a personal level. These people also have the ability to sense people's emotions and imagine what they might be thinking or feeling at a particular point in time. An empathetic leader can make his followers trust him blindly when they walk up to him for some form of emotional support. They don't even become hesitant confiding in him or revealing to him their secrets.

Then there is another leadership style referred to as ethical leadership. An ethical leader is well aware of the rules of behavior and makes sure his team members do the same. As a result, the workplace becomes happier and more morally sound.

Difference between Positive and Negative Attitudes

Up until now, we have discussed the significance of a positive attitude in a leader. We also discussed the different leadership styles and how they help a leader become successful. We haven't distinguished between a positive and a negative mental attitude. In the following paragraphs, we will take a look at some of the differences between a positive and a negative mental attitude.

An individual with a positive mental attitude always pays attention to the good in people, things, and situations. For example, even if this specific person isn't having a good day, he will appreciate the weather that he finds pleasant.

On the flip side, a person with a negative attitude always pays attention to bad things and completely ignores the good ones. In our lives, we come across people who are professionally sound, financially affluent, and possess a multitude of things they should be grateful for. However, somehow they end up focusing and stressing that one little thing that doesn't turn out the way they planned.

Let's take a look at some more differences between a positive and a negative mental attitude.

- A person with a positive attitude always focuses on opportunities. On the flip side, a person with a negative attitude tends to focus only on the downsides and limitations, depriving him of his ability to make the most out of his true potential which has been embedded in his default system.

- A person with a positive mental attitude sees the good in people. Not only does he appreciate the positive virtues in others, but he also tries to cultivate the same in himself. On the contrary, a person with a negative attitude only sees the loopholes in people who surround him. He spends so much time thinking about the shortcomings of others that he ends up developing the same in himself. The worst part is that he isn't aware of it.

- A positive attitude helps you identify the problems that might obstruct your path to success. But at the same time, it enables you to come up with solutions to those obstructions. As a result, you get your job done effectively and efficiently. However, the person with a negative attitude toward life focuses too much on the problems that he loses his problem-solving ability. In fact, his constant complaining and protest give birth to an entirely new problem.

- People with a positive mental attitude toward life set long-term goals and do whatever it takes to achieve those goals in a timely manner. Whereas people with a negative mental attitude toward life have a hard time setting goals. Even if they do end up setting a goal or two, they won't be able to go past the short-term goal mark, for the negativity in them will only haunt them while keeping them completely oblivious to the opportunities which they can make the most out of.

- People with a positive attitude have a strong conviction that things will eventually turn out in their favor. Therefore, they do not pay much attention to initial setbacks, nor do they scale their goals down. On the other hand, a person with a negative mental attitude believes that the only good things in life happened in the past, and in the future, he doesn't stand a chance to succeed. They have nothing major to look forward to, and therefore, they end up wasting their time and competencies; and when the realization kicks in, it has already been too late.

- A positive mental attitude is not only crucial to success, but it also fills us up with the right kind of emotions such as love, hope, joy, peace, and gratitude. These emotions are necessary for our mental and physical well-being and they minimize the chances of mental health problems such as depression, anxiety, and stress. On the flip side, a negative attitude paves the way for all the wrong emotions such as anger, envy, disappointment, and irritation. These emotions can open the doors to negativity, which can further lead to mental health issues, like the ones we have just spoken of.

How Does Attitude Affect Those around Us?

We meet numerous people daily. All of them have a different personality type, which is perfectly alright. However, some of those people are such that we find ourselves unintentionally smiling in their presence. Then some people only focus on the negative aspect of things. These are the people we try to avoid at all costs.

That's right; our attitude has a profound impact on the people in our surroundings. The only problem is that we don't understand the extent. There are times when we are around fun and energetic people. As a result, we find ourselves feeling more cheerful, and vice versa. Therefore, it is important to surround us with the people who uplift our mood, only to make us better versions of ourselves.

All of us have had the experience of working in environments where the boss isn't necessarily the nicest of characters. Such people have cold behaviors and a negative outlook on life. In their company, we rarely get a chance to grow and evolve as individuals. What they fail to realize is that their negative attitude not only hurts their team, but they also affect the performance of the entire organization. If you are in a position of power, you need to have an attitude you want to be replicated, and not the other way around.

If you want your work environment to be encouraging and motivating, you need to give off positive vibes to provide them with such an environment where everyone feels driven. As far as attitude is concerned, we tend to receive what we give. It is a two-way thing. Let's suppose you go to a grocery store and talk to the cashier with disrespect. He will probably treat us in the same way, rather than wishing us a nice day as we walk out. Similarly, your co-worker might not be the most cheerful of people, even if he isn't such a bad person to the core. But if you make a habit of greeting them every day in the morning and in the evening before checking out, a time will come when they will be the first ones to greet.

There are times when we aren't in a good mood. However, we do have the option to manage our moods. Some people have a habit of taking their frustration out on the people around them, which in some cases is forgivable. But it doesn't do us any good. Neither does it help us relieve the stress that we are feeling. The truth is that people will rarely notice if you are having a bad day or you are in a bad mood. But they will surely notice and they might react if we lash out at someone in anger or even convey displeasure toward a person or a thing that they did.

Even if you are feeling a little down, there are ways in which you can still show some respect to the people around you. It is not necessary for you to be feeling extremely happy 24/7, but the people we surround ourselves with are deeply impacted by our attitude, so it is better to keep it under control.

Here are a few things that you need to remember about having a positive attitude.

- On average, a person comes into contact with at least ten people daily. The only difference is that your attitude will not only affect those ten people. But it will have an impact on the dozens of people with whom these ten people come into contact. Therefore, you need to check your attitude and the kind of impact you are sending out.

- Your attitude also has a strong impact on your work behavior. With a positive mental attitude, not only will you work quicker, but the quality of your work will also be better. On the flip side, with a negative mental attitude, not only will you take longer to perform the simplest of tasks, but the quality of your work will also suffer.

- Moreover, your attitude doesn't reflect only in your words and actions. It also shows through your facial expressions, the way you stand, the way you walk, as well as the way you dress. Ironically, non-verbal cues can be far more severe and lasting compared to verbal ones.

- Moving on, your attitude has an impact on your health. It doesn't mean that people with a positive attitude never become sick or go to the hospital. However, people who stay optimistic have a higher likelihood of recovering from their health issues. On the other hand, people with a negative mindset succumb to their health issues completely and have a hard time recovering.

A Positive Attitude Can Be Contagious

"Attitude is a little thing that can make a big difference." **- *Winston Churchill***

One of the things that are constant in our lives is change. There are times when things don't go according to plan. That is when the negativity starts to kick in. These are the times when you are met with the worst obstructions that hinder your path. The good news is that your success or failure can only be determined through your attitude. Therefore, it is always helpful to move around with a positive mental attitude. This isn't the easiest thing to do, but it is quite possible. When the going gets tough, a lot of people snap, but that isn't very helpful. Instead, what you should do is to monitor your attitude throughout the process. If you realize that there is something off about your attitude, then you should change it straightaway.

It Helps You Take Challenges

A smooth life without any challenge or turbulence can be extremely dull and boring. Moreover, a life without challenges doesn't help you learn about yourself. It also keeps you from evolving. But the real challenge is to handle the problems that life throws at us. Interestingly, to deal with these challenges, one little thing that you need to tweak is your attitude. It can make a great difference. Changing your attitude is just a small turn of the screw, which can help you sail through a rough situation.

Adopting a Positive Mental Attitude

There are things in life that you can do and then there are things that you can't do. The only difference between the two things is your attitude. Moreover, your attitude isn't confined to some short-term or long-term goals, but it affects your entire life.

The motivation to improve your attitude can come from anywhere. There are some inside sources and some outside sources. The outside sources are mainly your friends, your peers, your role models, as well as some significant events that had an impact on your life.

Furthermore, the inner source of motivation is your inner self. It is very important to pay attention to the force that pushes you forward. One negative thought gives birth to another negative thought. The cycle continues and the same thing happens in the case of positive thoughts.

Gratitude and Leadership

One of the most crucial weapons inside a leader's toolkit is gratitude. It enables him to acknowledge and appreciate the efforts of his team members as well as his subordinates. As a result, he cultivates a team of driven and confident individuals who believe in their ability to succeed. On the flip side, a leader who isn't grateful is always judgmental of his team as well as the input that comes from them. Hence, an extremely demotivated and defeatist team comes into being. Moreover, such leaders gain little or no respect from their team, and it doesn't take long for their teams to disintegrate before their goals are accomplished.

A leader with gratitude helps you rise way above the image of a boss which has been embedded into our minds for quite some time and which in some cases is true. A grateful leader can cultivate long-term healthy relationships in his subordinates and teammates, which gives birth to trust. The more your team trusts you, the more respect you will gain as a leader. As a result, the flow of information will become easier and you won't even have a hard time explaining to them what to do and how it must be done.

Risk-Taking and Leadership

Everyone who has occupied a managerial position or a post where he is in charge of a group of people understands the significance of risk-taking. However, before discussing the importance of risk-taking in terms of leadership, we need to understand what risk-taking is. Simply put, risk-taking is anything that helps you escape the comfort zone. Speaking of comfort zones, they are very nice, warm, and comfortable places. But the only problem is that they are dry and barren places where everything seizes to grow. It doesn't matter whether your goals are big enough, you will have to step out of the dreaded comfort zone to achieve them.

Now let's come back to leadership. Risk-taking is crucial to the success of leadership and it doesn't end there. Risk-taking also plays a vital role in the personal lives of leaders. Now the extent of risk-taking is variable from one person to another, depending upon their age, nature, financial background, as well as academic and moral upbringing.

As we discussed earlier, a positive attitude is contagious. On the same measure, risk-taking is just as contagious. Furthermore, the contagiousness of risk-taking isn't limited to yourself. It is also inspirational to the people who look up to you. When your team members see you taking risks and moving forward in the direction of your goal, they are compelled to do the same. That is when you truly become successful.

With time, the culture of taking risks is on the rise. The people of today have understood that the consequences of risk-taking can be disastrous. Still, it opens us up to new opportunities. We need to realize that if we attempt to achieve something that we don't know much about, merely through our adventurism, the likelihood of failure goes up. However, this failure can present you with the mistakes you made as well as ways to troubleshoot your mistakes. Moreover, just because you have taken a risk, failed, and realized your shortcomings, it doesn't mean that the risk has been eliminated and it won't challenge you as you go forth. But after you have made a mistake and realized how this mistake should be eliminated, you start taking calculated risks, which often leads to success. Therefore, it can be said that risk-taking isn't a commodity that guarantees successful leadership. Instead, it is a step-by-step process that gets you through eventually and it needs a considerable amount of patience.

One of the questions that arise when someone talks about leadership is why risk-taking is important. Well, the answer is quite simple and straightforward. First of all, a leader who is out on a mission is driven to take risks. But if you haven't reached the pinnacle of influential and inspirational leadership, you are in luck. If you take risks, you will see an increase in the longevity of your time as a leader. Secondly, it opens you up to new and valuable experiences that can teach you what you can't learn in any classroom. It also opens you up to financial independence and stability, which you can utilize to fulfill your goal. Lastly, risk-taking provides you with a driven set of individuals to add to the team of individuals who will look up to you no matter what.

Fear is one of the primary reasons why people dread taking risks. The fact of the matter is that we are so hardwired to the status quo that the idea of putting ourselves out there sends shivers up our spines. However, the risks you take should be calculated. They should be backed by a sheer amount of research and homework, or else it would just be recklessness that doesn't take you anywhere. Here are some quick tips you can use to take calculated risks.

- Define your goals and always have a vision.
- Gather the necessary information.
- Compare your resources at hand with the possible costs.
- Make a habit of doing the things that scare you.
- Know your abilities and trust your decisions.
- Increase your emotional intelligence.

- Eliminate the negative people from your life and stay out of situations that put your mental peace at risk.
- Learn from the past, but don't grow in the past.
- Be prepared for rejection or failure.
- Learn to test your ideas and be reactive.
- Accept and embrace change, as it is the only constant thing.
- Don't try to be perfect and always remain flexible, but this flexibility should have some boundaries.

Leadership and the Holy Spirit

In the previous chapters, we have discussed how important it is for a leader to be close to Christ and the father. This quality helps you become kinder, wiser, and more compassionate. Sadly, some people take this straight to heart and leave their quest to become a leader, for they feel that just because they aren't spiritually inclined, they can't transform themselves into leaders, or so it seems. Contrary to popular belief, it is quite possible to transform into a leader, even if you don't have the Holy Spirit in you.

When you start turning into a leader, that is exactly when God starts to induce the Holy Spirit into you. The same thing happened in the case of Moses. This is what God said to Moses, *"Bring me seventy of Israel's elders who are known to you as leaders and officials among the people." (Numbers 11:16)*

It must be noted that these people were already leaders, but God put the divine spirit into them to help Moses in His mission.

"Carry the burden of the people" and he would "not have to carry it alone." (verse 17)

Some people believe that the spirit can leave the person after it is given to him from above. The truth is that the Holy Spirit is something that doesn't come and go very often. Once it is bestowed upon you, it will stay there. However, it is up to you whether or not you want to transfer some of it to the people who look up to you.

"I will take some of the Spirit that is on you and put it on them." (Numbers 11:17)

Another misconception that needs to be eliminated is that the leadership that is inspired by spirit has something fancy or flashy about it, whereas the reality is the exact opposite of what appears. If you have read and thought about the bible and the scriptures, you will understand the kinds of tasks assigned to Israel's leaders that God chose through Moses. However, if you don't, you might live with the misconception that they all were transformed into kings and men of power, but it didn't happen that way. God blesses His people in a way that is unforeseen to man. All those leaders of Israel were given the task of looking after the common people and fulfilling their day-to-day needs. For example, suppose you have reviewed the New Testament. In that case, you will know that Stephen was a leader chosen by God to look after the poor and helpless widows around him.

Furthermore, the people God chooses to be His chosen leaders are the ones who are spirited and wise. Unfortunately, in the world we live, we consider a person spirited and wise for all the wrong reasons. For example, if a person is a pro in conducting business through unlawful means and knows how to manipulate other people; similarly, if a person is in tune with the latest trends and knows how to carry, his fashion is considered spirited. We also judge a person's spirit through his success and his professional and academic accolades. But in the eyes of God, being spirited and wise is something different. In his eyes, the spirited and the wise person is calm, humble, compassionate, loving, kind, and doesn't ask for anything in return when he does nice things or contributes to the betterment of the people who surround him. Moreover, he doesn't become overwhelmed because of the challenges that are thrown their way.

Another aspect of spirit inspired leadership is servant leadership. A leader who carries with him the Holy Spirit bestowed upon him by his maker isn't the bossy type. Instead, he is humble, which transforms him into a person who works for the betterment of his followers and those around him. He is kind, loving, and compassionate. The best part is that he doesn't expect anything in return for the services he provides. Furthermore, through his acts of kindness, he wants to inspire those who look up to him, which sends him a step closer to God.

"Did not come to be served, but to serve." (Matthew 20:28)

A leader who is inspired by a spirit isn't only beneficial to the people around him, but his aspirations also have a profound impact on his personality and character. To become a leader, you don't need a lot of charisma and attraction. Those things are important, but if you are sincere and committed to your goal and your followers' well-being, you can quite easily go the distance, even if you aren't the flashiest person in the room. The spirit strengthens your character so that your only source of power is Jesus Christ and the father. Once you reach that stage, you cultivate in yourself a kind of charisma that doesn't come by very easily. Furthermore, this charisma is permanent and doesn't fade away with time.

Leader Confidence and How to Cultivate It

It doesn't matter whether a person is an influential leader or a leader with spirit, one thing that is unanimous among all leaders is confidence. Everyone wants to become more and more confident, but no one has the magic pill to cultivate confidence in how they walk, talk, and carry themselves. Some people are born extroverts. In their default system, it is to go about their lives, communicating and conducting business with a demeanor that exudes an aura of confidence. These people are liked and admired by the people who surround them, and even if they don't admit it, a lot of people secretly want to be like them. The interesting part is that some people tend to impersonate certain actions of these confident actions secretly in a subtle way, which is fine as long as it doesn't hurt them or any other individual. Then some people are a little introverted. For them, the real challenge arises. However, it doesn't necessarily mean that being an introvert should keep you from becoming a leader. In the following paragraphs, we will share a few ways that will help you cultivate the kind of confidence that you need to transform yourself into an inspirational and influential leader.

- **Go Back to School**: It is a fact that confidence comes through hands-on experience of a particular thing or a situation. But suppose you are too scared to put yourself out there. In that case, you can resort to some academia to help you get the hang of what confidence means and how people have used it to their advantage. You can take courses online or from the local institute or college near your place. You can listen to motivational speeches by some of the most renowned speakers of the day, such as Tony Robbins. You can also resort to a few self-help books that are trending on the internet. If you attend a motivational trainer session, try to hang out with them for a while after the session is over. Also, read about the great leaders who have walked the face of the earth. Martin Luther King can be a good point to start. The more you learn about confidence, the easier it will be for you to become a confident individual and a confident leader one day.

- **Network with Leaders**: Congratulations, you have put the first step forth. Now you are going out of your way to learning about leaders. Pat yourself on the back for mustering up the courage to break the comfort zone. But it still is a long way to go. Just because you are reading up on leadership doesn't mean that a motivational session or a ted talk will transform you overnight. You still need to step out and face your fears. Mistakes are meant to be made, but these mistakes can be worthwhile if you learn from them and never commit them again. Most importantly, surround yourself with people who are on the same mission as you are. Not only will it give you a sense of belongingness, but it will also make you feel that you aren't alone in this quest and that some people are in the same place as you are.

- **Cultivate Self-Awareness**: The next thing you need to do is become more self-aware. This is good for two reasons. First of all, it helps you realize your strengths and opens you up to your weaknesses and things that you can do to improve yourself. Make sure you seek feedback from the people you surround yourself with. Plus, asking for feedback will help you appear as a more confident individual in people's eyes, which will end up working in your favor. However, it is essential who the feedback is coming from. It should come from brutally honest people and not the ones who avoid rocking the boat with the sweetest things to say. Although bitter, the former feedback will help you grow and develop yourself into a more assertive version of yourself.

- **Help Others**: Contrary to popular belief, leadership confidence has nothing to do with being self-righteous and full of yourself. Moreover, a person who is full of himself can only become a boss and not a leader. He is too busy obsessing over and talking about his accolades that he has no time left to motivate others. It is useful if you have to tell your personal stories of success to motivate your followers. A leader spends more time and energy resources to help others become more successful. Help your followers cultivate self-awareness, thus enabling them to embark on a journey of becoming leaders themselves.

- **Celebrate Victories**: Another quality of a great leader is that he inspires his followers to become high achievers. In doing so, he uses the concept of positive reinforcement. For example, if one of your teammates hits a milestone, make sure to let them know how thrilled you are because they are successful. You can take them out to lunch or throw a party to celebrate their achievement. This will make them realize that there is someone who genuinely cares about their performance. So, the next time you assign them a big project, they will have much more to look for, rather than mere completion of the project.

- **Get in Shape**: Alright, up until now, we have spoken about how leadership has to do with what's inside you and not your outer covering. That's right, as a leader, you need to give your followers a lot more to love about you other than your sincerity and commitment to your work and team. It would also help if you made them admire you physically. Be very particular about the way you dress. Make sure you maintain your wardrobe and not show up to work wearing the same clothes you have been wearing for the past week. Similarly, try hitting the gym or going for a jog a few times a weak. This will help you stay in shape and you will feel more confident about yourself. Furthermore, working out, jogging, and playing physical sports release certain hormones in your brain, which help you feel better and more confident about yourself. Make sure to maintain your facial hair. Either shave off the whole thing or grow a beard and make sure to trim it after a few days to keep it in shape. Your footwear should be simple yet clean. Interestingly, your shoes have a profound impact on the people you meet. Also, you should smell nice. It is okay to put on a lot of deodorants, but you should shower every day. You can even resort to mild perfume.

- **Stand Tall**: Another thing you must do to transform yourself into a confident leader is to stand tall and have a confident body posture. We don't necessarily realize it, but our body posture, body language, and the way we carry ourselves significantly impact our lives. The taller we stand, the better we feel about ourselves, as well as our ability to make decisions and stand by them. You must always keep your chin up and send a message to the world that you will not succumb, no matter what is thrown your way. A confident body posture is something that doesn't come overnight. It is the final finishing of a spiral of things that you do. There are so many building blocks to a healthy and confident body posture. First of all, you should ensure that you get at least six to eight hours of uninterrupted sleep every night. Secondly, be very careful about what goes into your stomach because, after all, you are what you eat. If you feel weak, visit the doctor and make up for your shortcomings with some supplements and multivitamins. Furthermore, work out regularly and be very particular about what you wear and how you carry it. If you are confident in your skin, it will be much easier for you to be a source of inspiration to those who follow you.

- **Make Friends**: Next up, try to make new friends. It can be a little hard if you are an introvert who doesn't like meeting people daily. If you are addicted to your comfort zone, it becomes even more dangerous. The good thing is that you can step out of the dreaded place. Start slow and make a habit of meeting at least one new person every week. Ask them questions about themselves and make sure you listen very carefully to what they have to say. Don't be too picky when choosing a person. Always keep your heart open. This is good for two reasons. First of all, it will help you overcome your fear of breaking the ice with a stranger. Secondly, it will tell you a lot about people and their nature, which will help lead people when given a chance. Try to talk to your new-found friends one on one, rather than calling them, emailing them, or communicating with them through a video call. The pleasure of connecting with another human is too great, especially if you have been isolating yourself for quite some time. Real interactions give you positive energy, which cannot be found anywhere else.

- **Be the Servant**: This is a continuation of the concept of servant leadership that we have discussed many paragraphs earlier. To become a great leader, you need to serve first. This doesn't mean that you have to go from one house to another and do the dishes or rub floors. However, if you are a servant, you strive for others' betterment, which makes you feel better about yourself. Furthermore, when you do something kind for someone and they are grateful, your body releases oxytocin, which gives you a warm and fuzzy feeling, thus making you want to commit more acts of kindness. When people know that you have done something nice for them without asking for anything in return, they become gratuitous and start looking up to you as their leader.

- **Build a Repute:** Lastly, to develop the confidence to become a leader, you should build a strong reputation. Now, it is totally up to you how you want to be remembered. If you want to be remembered as a good person, you need to do a few easy things. First of all, you should be honest. Secondly, you should keep your promises. Every time you make a promise, follow it through right till the very end and do not shy away or break it, for it will come at the expense of your reputation. Similarly, always be honest, even if it can create a few problems for you. At least, through honesty, you can avoid bigger problems down the road.

Chapter 5: Pastoral Leadership

Some people who are new to the idea of pastoral leadership somehow believe that pastors are creatures that belong to some other planet and the traits that they possess are quite inhuman. Alright, this is just a little exaggerated, but some people have similar approaches to what it means to be a pastoral leader. We must remember that pastors and preachers are just normal living and breathing human beings, with the same emotions, feelings, and thoughts as everyone else has. Even though they are God's chosen people that He has appointed to carry His message forth, they are absolute individuals with unique and distinct personalities. The interesting part about their uniqueness is that it doesn't collide with the church's values. Instead, their distinctiveness and diversity are healthy for the establishment and the sustainability of the church ministry.

Suppose you think or talk from the ministry's standpoint. In that case, you need to have a rock-solid grip on pastoral leaders' different personality types. By doing so, you will allow yourself to look deeper into pastors and preachers' personalities. Therefore, you will keep yourself from getting caught in common weaknesses, which are present in pastoral leaders. Moreover, it will enable you to zero in on their personalities' strengths, rather than being too obsessed with their weaknesses.

Similarly, you need to think about your personality, weaknesses, and strengths. This creates self-awareness. In the process, you realize that you can use things to increase the proximity between yourself and God, thus arriving at an almost exaltingly pastoral position.

If you delve deep, you will come to know that every pastor is a combination of several personality traits. However, one of those several traits is predominant. None of the leadership styles is better than the other. Each pastoral leadership style has its strengths, which the pastor can use to influence and inspire the people who follow them. In the following paragraphs, we will look at the different pastoral leadership styles and the strengths they have to offer. So, without further ado, let's get down to business.

Theologian

The theologian is a student of the things the scriptures have to offer. At the same time, he is the master of all the things which have a doctrinal disposition. A theologian is very smart. If you meet any, you will realize that they have a firm grip even over the tiniest of details revealed in the scriptures. Unlike their comrades, the theologians are rather introverted. They like to stay in their space without too much human interaction. But this seclusion allows them to practice strong self-discipline. Their confidence and knowledge are a great source of inspiration for those who look up to them and seek their guidance in religious matters.

Teacher

As the word suggests, a teacher has traits that are similar to that of a theologian. But the difference between a teacher and a theologian is that a teacher isn't quite well-versed when it comes to doctrinal matters. With that being said, it doesn't mean that teachers don't have a firm grasp of the doctrine. However, studying doctrines and coming up with interpretations isn't their forte. In today's fast-paced times, the teacher's role has been reduced to something quite insignificant, but the part they play isn't far from the literal truth. It is part of a teacher's job to finish a business that has been left unfinished by others. Therefore, they bridge a crucially important gap. Some teachers are introverted and are mistaken for theologians, but the difference is that they aren't introverted all the time and exhibit such behaviors occasionally.

Authoritarian

Yes, you guessed it quite right — the authoritarian pastor has a fairly strong, outgoing, and extroverted personality. Furthermore, authoritarian pastoral leaders have a top-to-bottom mindset. These people are strong and have stronger willpower than others. They are extremely confident and known for their excellent decision-making. Furthermore, even if their decisions aren't the best, they dare to stand by them, right till the very end.

They don't take failure to heart. Instead, they look at mistakes as opportunities and a means to move forward. These people can distinguish between right and wrong. They also possess the courage to speak up when they see something wrong happening around them, even if they are aware of the fact that their courageousness can put them in a lot of trouble. They are committed to the work of God, and therefore, they are always willing to abide by God's teachings, even if it comes at the expense of risking their skin. To them, respect is the greatest gift, but they don't want it to come at the cost of someone else's dishonor. They are helpers and like to pick others up as well as encourage them to improve and be better at whatever they do.

These were just a handful of the several pastoral leadership types. It would be wrong to say that a particular leadership type is better than the other. All pastoral leaders are unique, depending on their leadership style. They have their areas of expertise. They all are comprehensive institutions in themselves, with something different to bring to the table. However, one thing that is unanimous among all these people is that they are utterly sincere to the church's ministry and the things that it stands for. To them, the fulfillment of God's will is the greatest priority. For that purpose, they are willing to do whatever it takes. They inspire others to do the same.

Pastors as Servant Leaders

One of the biggest problems with the ministries in our times is that pastors have a hard time maintaining the balance between being a leader and a servant. They often ask whether or not it is possible to be a leader and a servant at the same time, for the two terms used with one other are rather an oxymoron. The question that pops up in the minds of the people is valid and should be answered. The problem is that people look for easy answers without putting in the hard work needed, but the reality is that there are no easy answers. However, if you consider the example of Jesus, you might come across a satisfactory answer. The way Jesus trained His followers and disciples for the ministry gave birth to a whole new leadership style.

"Jesus went out to a mountainside to pray and spent the night praying to God. When morning came, He called His disciples to Him and chose twelve of them, whom He also designated apostles." Luke 6:12, 13

One thing that should be noted is that Jesus didn't gather a large following overnight. Instead, a significant amount of prayer and thought went into the entire process of gathering a group of people and training them for the ministry. To the outside world, these people lack the slightest bit of glamor and sheen, but Jesus didn't hire them for some worldly success. He hired them for the innocence and the simplicity that he sensed in them. He understood very well that these were the people who would stand by His side even in the toughest of times and they would go forth to lead others.

The time these people spent with Jesus was a life-changing experience for them. It wouldn't be wrong to say that Jesus was an instrument that God used to bring these lost souls into the fold of faith. Jesus treated them not like His servants but His children and did everything in His power to make them stay with Him right till the very end. He spent time with them, showed them sympathy, and took care of their most trivial needs. As a result, these people fell in love with the man, and it got to the point where they were willing to go the distance. He wasn't cruel or strict with His approach. That is part of the reason why He succeeded. Instead, He took the path of forgiveness and, therefore, inspired His followers to transform into dynamic leaders who would go forth and spread the word of God to the people.

At the same time, Jesus was well aware of the fact that he lived in the real world, which isn't always the friendliest of places. He could sense that the pressure exerted from the outside world would scare His followers into leaving the path of God. He made them realize that despite the hardships they faced, the future would have something great in store for them and their future would certainly be happier and more joyous than the present. He told them that a great era was just at their threshold, and these were the men who would make it all happen if they stood together by their mission, and did not flinch, regardless of what was thrown their way.

The People's Leader

Jesus is by far one of the most extraordinary leaders the world has ever seen. He wasn't just a program leader, which is exactly something people expect from a person who is out on the mission to inspire a group of individuals to achieve a certain objective. Let's break it down into two different points.

- First of all, He invested His entire life in His followers. He ate, slept, worked, and even traveled with them. It wouldn't be wrong to say that the relationship He shared with His disciples was similar to that of a big brother with his younger siblings.

- Secondly, he believed in them and offered them the best. For a leader, the hardest part is to trust His team members, for he is uncertain whether or not His team members would carry His mission forth. The way He asks them to make disciples of all nations clearly shows how much He trusted them and believed in them.

The motivation of His leaders also didn't develop overnight. Instead, it was a step-by-step process, which took some time. Here is a breakdown.

- First of all, they developed a loving identity with him.
- They grew a significant amount of love and respect not only for the man but also for the cause that He stood for.
- Lastly, they adopted His teachings and preachings and almost became an attitude for them - a way of life, to be exact.

Servant Leadership

One of the problems with Christian leadership is that it isn't deeply rooted in the model of servanthood that Jesus gave birth to. On one occasion, He asked, "What can I do for my people?" He could have asked, "What can my people do for me?" but He didn't. Such a model requires a sheer amount of humility and sacrifice, and therefore, it is easier said than done. That is part of the reasons why not many people adopt it and incorporate it into their approach. However, they fail to realize that the results of such an approach are long-lasting. Moreover, we live in a materialistic world. A person following this model will be taken for granted. His teachings won't be given the stature that they deserve.

To become a servant leader like Jesus, you need to develop a lot of acceptance. You should accept and tolerate people for the way they are. From there, you can work on them, thus shaping them into the character that you want them to be. The thing that Jesus' disciples knew very well was that to be accepted, they didn't have to be rich and successful. He forgave all of their mistakes, showered on them unconditional love, and kept their self-respect intact. His servant leadership style is the reason why they trusted Him blindly and were willing to follow Him everywhere.

Sustaining This Leadership Style

Here are some easy tips for sustaining the servant leadership style.

- Try to transform people. This takes time, but through rigorous effort, you can make it.
- Do not jump the gun. Introduce one change at a time.
- Cultivate extremely optimistic group dynamics.
- Impart new values through love and not strictness.
- Practice open communication with your team, so there are no secrets.
- Don't try to take everything into your hands. Delegate responsibility.

Church Growth Strategies in the 21st Century

Let's suppose you are a pastor or a priest. You should be aware that God wants to see the church grow, He has chosen you as His servant, and He wants you to play your part in the development of the church. Not only does He want you to serve the church, but the number of lives that you change and improve in the process also brings Him immense pleasure. All you have to do is take the initiative, and He will send His support in ways you cannot even foresee.

For some people, the topic of church growth is interesting and theoretical to talk about. However, there is more to that than just theory. While many churches are coming into existence, at the same time, the opposite is also true. There are also churches closing down, which is a very sad thing to witness, especially for the believers who want to see the churches grow and evolve. For example, in the year 2014, more than 3,500 churches were shut down, but the good news is that at the same time, there were around 4,000 new churches that came into being.

There is one thing that not many people understand, which is why they have a hard time keeping churches intact. Whether it is a new church, a church that has hit the point of stagnation, or a booming church, the needs of a church are unanimous. So, how can one play his part in the growth of a church? If this question pops up in your head, you are not alone. If you go through the numbers, you will realize that there are more than 2,000 searches on Google every month, in which people look for church growth strategies. They also search for ways to increase the number of people who attend the church regularly.

In the following paragraphs, we will share some easy tips that will enable you to help a church grow, considering the troubled times that we are living in today. However, before we move forward, you should take a look at some of the church growth myths that we have listed below.

Church Growth Myths

Maybe God is inspiring your church through evangelism and a great outreach or growth is a practical imperative. Regardless of what your reasons for growth are, there is a perspective reset that you need. So, let's look at it this way. What you want is a great harvest, but before you achieve that, you will have to remove the loose soil and the dry plants and their roots. Until and unless the wastes are removed, you won't be able to bag the harvest, regardless of your seeds' quality and the fertilizer you use. In the same measure, before you see the church blossom and attract a considerable amount of believers in its fold, you will have to get rid of the negativity that tends to float around in the form of myths and misconceptions, just like the ones we have mentioned below. So, let's break it down.

Myth # 1: Growth Alludes to a Healthy Church

There is no denying the fact that healthy things continue to grow. However, not many people pay attention to the fact that unhealthy things grow too. Just because the growth isn't apparent doesn't mean that it isn't there. When it comes to church growth, most people only focus on the size, which is fine, but size isn't the only thing that matters. All across the globe, we see high and mighty churches that tell fascinating stories about their growth. However, after some time, we hear in the news that the same church imploded and died down and now it is shut down. This happens because the people in charge pay too much attention to what is outside rather than what is inside. If only they focus on creating and implementing God's growth strategies, there'd be so many churches in the world that would have been operating still, but they are gone now. Strengthening the church from within is what lasts, while the look and the image are temporary. It is perfectly alright if you want to remodel your church and make it appear big, but remember that your church's size doesn't guarantee growth and success.

Myth # 2: It Is the Poor Leadership That Makes a Church Fail

One of the most pivotal factors crucial to the growth of a church is a strong, stable, and devout leadership. The pastors and the priests should try their best to keep the church intact and play their part in its growth. Even though pastors have some significant responsibilities on their shoulders, it doesn't mean that it is the pastor's fault if the church fails to grow. It could be, but there are more reasons for the failure of the church than poor leadership. The world that we live in places so much burden on the pastors. They take it upon themselves to deliver and not disappoint the people who look up to them. This is why some pastors develop mental health issues, for they cannot absorb any more pressure and some of them even end up seeking therapy. We need to understand that several internal and external factors are at work when a ministry grows, even if we can't see them. The church leadership shouldn't be blamed solely.

In most cases, when a church fails to grow, the first person to be blamed is the pastor, and this is a very dangerous trend that should definitely change for good. Some churches even go the extra mile, making the horrendous mistake of having the pastor replaced. The results are shocking, as most churches fail to recover. Some of them even collapse, never to be established again. With that being said, we should remember that pastors are human beings and they too can make mistakes, but the mistakes they make aren't too big to have them replaced with someone new.

Myth # 3: Church Growth Depends upon Holidays

It is a fact that holidays such as Easter and Mother's Day bring a considerable amount of traffic to your church, which might appear as an omen of growth, but that is just a very myopic approach that is far away from reality. Providing excellent services on holidays to your visitors can work in your favor, but there is a lot more that you can do. For better outreach, you should cultivate a culture that compels people to visit the church all year round. Holidays may present you with great opportunities, but most of the growth is lost during the remaining part of the year if you fail to keep up. You should come up with church-wide habits and attitudes that compel your occasional visitors to turn into regular visitors, so you can enjoy a non-stop inflow of traffic throughout the year.

Now that we have spoken about the church growth myths, let's shift gears and get down to business. In the upcoming paragraphs, we will talk about some of the strategies you can use to grow your church. So, let's break it down.

Say "No" to All Distractions

While discussing the growth myths, we spoke about the harvest and its importance to get rid of the loose soil and the waste plants. Similarly, it is very important to eliminate all sorts of distractions that obstruct your church's growth. So, your church has limited bandwidth. If you are too busy with the things that do not resonate with your church's mission and vision statements, it is better to have them taken out of the equation. Furthermore, you will never look at them the same way you look at your goals and objectives. Therefore, you will end up wasting your time without any significant return. However, it is very important to say yes to the right opportunities to help your church grow. But if you are the pastor or the person in charge, you need to be able to distinguish between opportunities and distractions.

Come Up with a Simple Mission Statement

It is very important to have a mission statement. The mission statement isn't only important for the church, but it is also crucial for the entire community. It provides a commonly shared goal to the community, which can gather around it and play its part in the betterment and growth of the church. One of the many problems that obstruct the church's growth is that the mission statements are annoyingly big and complex. Instead, they should be short and easy to understand.

Create Invitation Forms to Increase Your Traffic

There is nothing wrong with a little innovation that compels people to attend the church more often. The best thing you can do is come up with cute invitation cards that are easy to read and elegantly designed. It won't cost too much, but at the same time, it will add to your outreach. Speaking of innovation, ever since the internet and smartphones have become an integral part of our lives, they have revolutionized almost everything. Technology can benefit church groups in a very major way, but the unfortunate part is that not many people have utilized it to their advantage. However, very slowly, they are digitalizing their efforts, which will make things easier in the future. All you need do is to come up with a mobile application for your church. Your targeted groups will install this app on their phones and remain updated on the new initiatives.

Invest in the Youth

The fraction of the society that a church needs to influence the most is the youth, but that hasn't been happening a lot, which is a very dangerous trend. Some people who aren't very religious in their teens grow to become parents who are a little concerned about their children's religious education. This is a dilemma for the parents, but for the church, it is an opportunity. If you are a pastor who wants his church to flourish, make sure you develop initiatives specifically for the youth. This task is easier said than done. Therefore, it is in your best interest to appear extremely organized and confident in your approach. If you are successful in bringing the youth on board, make sure you conduct background checks. You can even get in touch with their parents if the need arises.

Invest in Smaller Groups

Some of the things you will hear the most at a church revolve around the community's transformational power. But this is far from reality, for the congregation's actions are quite different than the promises they make, and no one really delivers. The everyday gathering at the church is great, but it doesn't have the potential needed to work toward the unity of the entire Christian community. Therefore, before you embark on bigger goals, you must invest in smaller groups, which are bound together strongly. These smaller groups can focus better on their work, thus inspiring the outsiders to join in.

Free Coffee

Serving free coffee at the neighborhood bus stop is something not many people do, but it surely helps the church. It requires little investment, but this countercultural effort goes a long way. You can also give them a cookie or any other baked good, along with a note that signifies the importance of going to church. You can even print your church's name on the coffee cups.

Pastors Building Team for the Ministry

If you are a pastor, you can understand the significance of building a team. In the absence of a group of like-minded individuals, a pastor can find himself extremely confused and unable to perform his tasks. Building a team for the ministry isn't one of the easiest things to do. However, there are some simple steps that you can follow as a pastor to gather a team of people who can serve the ministry well, some of which are as follows.

Knowing Yourself

To build a team of individuals who are willing to go the distance for the ministry, you need to be completely aware of who you truly are. If you don't know yourself, your dream of formulating and training a team of devout individuals will remain a dream, and it will never see the light of day. Self-awareness is tough, but the easiest thing you can do in this regard is to focus on your strengths. This will enable you to gather a group of people with qualities that complement your own. You don't have to go out of your way looking for people who have the same strengths as yours. You only have to look for people who compliment you. Some people make the mistake of hiring people similar to them, which isn't a very intelligent thing to do. It may work for a short while, but in the long run, it will make your team terribly lopsided. Just because every individual on the team is alike, it will give birth to such gaps that are hard to fill, and in extreme cases, impossible.

The team that you hire should be diverse so that each individual's strengths are celebrated. You are bad at doing several things or you simply don't like doing. If you hire someone exactly like yourself, there will be a void that is impossible to fill. Let's suppose you are an outgoing person who is exceptionally well at public dealing, but you despise sitting in a room going through piles and piles of paperwork. Just because you don't have a liking for going through heaps of papers doesn't mean that it is necessary and should be put on a backburner. Therefore, you should look for someone who has a penchant for handling certain tasks that you aren't very good at. That is the reason that the person you should know most of all is yourself.

Determination of the Essential Church Ministries

There are so many churches that tend to have more ministries than the number of people needed to finance the church. Most churches try to have more than ten ministries when they need not more than five. By trying too hard, they end up depriving themselves of their ability to manage. If you are stuck in such a situation, the smart thing would be to identify the ministries you need and the ones that you can manage. By failing to give each ministry an equal amount of attention, you will be doing a sheer amount of injustice to your work, which will add pressure onto your shoulders. If you are directly leading a group of people, you may choose the ministry well. On the flip side, if your church is big enough, you won't be doing the management part on your own. Instead, you will be in an oversight role.

In such situations, you will be responsible for hiring assistant pastors and training them. Suppose you are pastoring a relatively smaller church. In that case, you will be responsible for all the shepherding tasks other than the pulpit ministry. Therefore, you will need to depend upon lay leadership to oversee the remaining aspects of the ministry. In a smaller church, lay leadership can be of great significance.

Before you hire a group of people who will assist you in your job, you need to determine the roles and responsibilities first. Sometimes, you will have to mold a specific role for a person rather than molding them to fulfill certain responsibilities.

Development of a Clearly Written Job Description

Now that you have hired a team of people, what's next? What is it exactly that you want each and every team member to do? You need to ask yourself about the skills that your team members possess. Furthermore, what will the weekly tasks be for each team member? You can never hire a team of people if you are completely oblivious to what each of them is going to do.

First of all, you need some clarity. Start by formulating a well-thought and well-written job description. Not only will it help you hire the right people, but it will also keep you from hiring the ones who don't necessarily fulfill your requirements. That would be the last thing that you would want, for that person would only be a liability. If you hire a person who doesn't fit the role, you will only be frustrating and stressing yourself even more. With a clearly defined job description, the newly appointed individual will have a vivid idea of what they need to do and the things that will make them eligible for the post. One of the many reasons why some people fail at their jobs is that they haven't the slightest bit of idea about what their role requires.

Hiring Team Players

It is very important for the newly hired people to possess the skills needed for their role. But do you know what's more important? The team members that you hire for the ministry should be team players. So, who exactly is a team player? A team player is the one who has the desire to succeed and wants his teammates to succeed. He helps them with whatever He has. It wouldn't be wrong to say that a ministry is a bit like a sports team where the star players put their best foot forth. However, in competitive sports, star performers tend to fight for individual recognition and glory. They aren't much concerned with their team members, as long as they are in the spotlight. These individuals can be celebrated as excellent athletes, but when it comes to teamwork, they won't be able to pass with flying colors. The people you hire for the ministry should value their team's interest before anybody else's. Selfishness, greed, jealousy, and envy should be discouraged at all costs when you are hiring people for the ministry.

The Development of Each Team Member

Lastly, it should be your utmost priority as a leader to help your team develop and grow. Doing so, you should provide each and every team member with support, guidance, and instructions. The worst thing you can do is assume that your team members will learn and grow on their own. Instead, you must make sure they grow and evolve as individuals who can serve the ministry in a very effective manner.

One of the simplest things you can do is organize weekly team meetings. It doesn't have to be very strict. It can be a mellow and chilled-out meetup where every team member should be allowed to voice their feelings and opinions about specific issues. If necessary, you can also arrange one-on-one meetings with your team members to evaluate their performance and make sure whether or not everything is going up to par. If there are any loopholes, you can always fill them with your skill and experience.

Such initiatives will help your staff members become more comfortable with you. Hence, they will open up to you, which will obliterate the communication barrier. Also, make sure to provide them with the right training and resources to do their job effectively and efficiently. Also, do not forget to provide them with lots of encouragement. The more they feel appreciated, the better performers they will become and work in favor of your ministry in the long run.

Chapter 6: Challenges of leadership

One of the biggest issues with the world around us is that people aren't willing to face enough challenges. Every time a tough situation gives a knock on the door, these people either shy away or tend to play the blame game, trying to absolve themselves of any kind of responsibility. At the same time, everybody daydreams about being a leader. Not many people are aware that one needs to go through some tough ordeals before being eligible to lead a group of people.

Some of them believe that just because you have been placed in a position of leadership and authority, nothing will go wrong. Contrary to popular belief, the real challenges occur when you are responsible for leading a group of individuals who look up to you for almost everything. However, this shouldn't scare you. The good news is that everything in life happens for a reason. Maybe if you have been picked up for a leadership role in any scenario, it must be because you have an inbuilt ability to lead.

As a leader, one of the things that you need to make friends with is change. When you are a leader, there are some changes that fate throws your way. You have to learn to adapt to those changes. Then, there are some changes that you bring about not only in your life but also in the world that surrounds you, and if you don't, you are forced to make those changes, and that is exactly how nature works.

In either of the two scenarios, you have to be flexible enough to mold yourself into a version that can fit perfectly in the given circumstances. Secondly, you have to put your faith in God and His ability to show you the right path every time you find yourself a little stuck. You should completely understand that if you want to succeed and change things for the better, you have to make some adjustments, which is the only way forward. If something is troubling you for a short while, let it pass, for that is the thing that will transform you into a better and stronger version of yourself.

Difficult People

It is a fact that no matter where you are, who you are, and what you are doing, there will always be some people around you who are difficult to deal with. However, as a leader, this can be a very challenging situation for you. First of all, you need those around, for each of them brings something unique to the table. Secondly, you can't just disconnect from them all of a sudden. It is your job to find a way to handle these people. However, make sure never to feed these people with what you have to offer. At the same time, do not let them control you and bring down the world on your head. There will be people in your team who are tough to work with. You should give them ample room, but at the same time, you should be calling the shots at the end of the day.

Pressuring Situations

If your work environment is pressure-free, consider yourself lucky. However, it could also allude to a mistake on your part or that of your teammate. Pressure is an integral component of a work environment. Its absence can lead to sudden failure. Suppose you and a group of people are on a mission to do something. In that case, you should expect some pressure. It is your job as the leader to accept that pressure and release it from time to time. It is your job to find ways to release some of the added pressure. It is humanly impossible to keep running at 100 miles an hour and hope that a miracle moment will give a knock on the door.

Letting People Go

As a leader, one of the hardest things to do is to let someone go. There are people in your organization who have been with you through the thick and thin. For some reason, letting them go is the best thing you can do. Sometimes, bidding farewell to an old colleague or a teammate with whom you have spent a significant portion of your life isn't the easiest of things. However, you have to do that, for there is no option left and no way forward. It is alright to let people go, for you can always find better and improved resources, as the market is brimming with them.

However, you must not take any decision in a hurry or in anger and frustration. Instead, it is in your best interest to deal with such issues in the calmest and relaxed way possible, for if you don't, you can scar your organization in a way that it becomes tough for you and your organization to recover.

Breaking Bad News

Often, you come up with new plans, new ideas, and even some new products and services. That is very brave of you, but at the same time, it doesn't mean that the new initiative will click, and you might even end up in a failure, which can be heart-wrenching, considering the amount of work you have put into it. But do you know what is even more difficult than to digest a failure? The real difficult part is when you have to break the news to your teammates, subordinates, and superiors. For there, it is totally up to you how you handle it. You can be extremely dramatic and mess everything up by allowing your emotions to take the best of you. The best thing to do is to break the bad news clearly and vividly and try not to get too carried away. You need to explain to others the reason behind your failure and how you can work hand in hand with your team to clean up the mess, which can be troublesome for the time being. If you follow the latter approach, people will give a significant amount of importance to your words and you will find yourself in a better position to troubleshoot the reasons behind the failure.

Staying Motivated

Even though God has made you a leader and bestowed some responsibilities on you, it doesn't mean that you seize to be a human. It is perfectly alright for a leader to feel a little demotivated. However, your job is to make sure the demotivation doesn't get to you. What you should do in these circumstances is to focus on your successes rather than failures. At the same time, you must look around yourself for inspiration and you might even find some.

Now, absorb all of that positive energy inside you and get back on track. If your intentions are clear, you will get back on track in no time. As a human being, you can't control everything, for not everything is meant to be within your reach, so it is better to leave those things the way they are and not spend any more time thinking about them. One more thing you should do as a leader is to appear as if you are the most enthusiastic person around. This will enable you to keep the team on track and galvanize them when the situation calls for it.

Cultural Problems

One of the most integral parts of an organization is the culture, which you have to abide by. Suppose you are working in an organization. It doesn't necessarily mean that you have to like everything about the culture. The chances are that you might have issues with the culture, which is absolutely alright. Sometimes, you might have an issue with your superiors, while sometimes the subordinates' behavior might not be to your liking. Whatever the situation is, you will have to deal with the cultural problems in an intelligent manner.

Changing the cultural habits within an organization might not be the easiest of things to do, but as a leader, it is your responsibility to set the tone. You have to lead by example. For example, if you have an issue with gossiping or backbiting, try to conduct an introspection and find out if those problems exist in your personality. If they do, make sure to throw them out right away. Suppose the people around you look up to you. In that case, they will surely try to imitate your behavior and attitude toward your colleagues. Therefore, you will find it much easier to mold the culture in an acceptable way to you. Similarly, if you want your team members to cooperate with you, you need to be a cooperative person yourself first.

Whether it is a nation, a community, or an organization, leadership is extremely important. To make important and large-scale decisions and keep things rolling, leaders are needed. One of the biggest problems with our society is that people are too eager to look for the bad in a leader. They never really take the time to identify the right one. There is an even better alternative to going out in search of leadership. Wouldn't it be better if people understand the traits a leader needs to incorporate into their persona and get things going? Absolutely. Therefore, we have put together a list of traits that a person needs to become a leader.

Integrity

One of the most important things that a person needs to become a leader is integrity. Yes, it can be a key metric as far as employee evaluation is concerned, but it is definitely important as far as the organization and the individuals are concerned. Furthermore, when hiring senior officers within the organizational hierarchy, integrity should be a standard of measurement, for the people on the top are the ones calling the shots and making all the important decisions. If you are the person in charge within a company, make sure you hire individuals with integrity and also lead by example to help your employees learn the blessed trait.

Delegating Ability

A leader cannot become a leader until and unless he possesses the ability to delegate responsibilities and duties. However, the delegation of responsibilities is not an easy thing to do. Some people occupying key positions in the organizational hierarchy tend to assign certain duties and responsibilities to their subordinates. By doing so, they try to reduce the burden of work on their shoulders. This is not how it should be done. The person calling the shots should be good at the delegation of responsibilities, but at the same time, they should demand regular reports from their teammates and subordinates. It will definitely provide them with a better picture of whether or not everything is up to par. At the same time, it will also put them in a better position to make better decisions, which will create a win-win situation for the organization and the people involved.

Effective Communication

It is better not to put a person in a leadership position before he cultivates the ability to communicate with different people on different levels within the organizational hierarchy. Not only does effective communication help you communicate valuable information to your teammates and subordinates, but it also enables a person to coach and train the people who look up to them when it comes to making important decisions. Furthermore, contrary to popular belief, communication is a two-way thing. If you want people to listen to you, you should also listen to them and pay the utmost attention to what they have to offer. In most cases, effective listening is much better than talking, for it opens you up to new ideas, possibilities, and opportunities.

Gratitude

Just step back, relax, take a deep breath, and ask yourself a simple question. What is it that distinguishes between a leader and a boss? The answer is simple and straightforward. The thing that differentiates between the two is gratitude. Furthermore, gratitude toward your team members and subordinates not only leads to better performance and organizational success, but there is more to that. When you are thankful for the things that others do for you, you end up benefitting yourself. Gratuitous people have a lesser likelihood of developing depression, anxiety, and sadness. It also helps you sleep better.

Self-Awareness

This attribute is extremely inwardly focused, but it is paramount to leadership. The better a person can understand himself, the better he can understand others, and the two parties can work in collaboration toward a commonly shared goal. It also opens you up to your weaknesses, strengths, threats, and opportunities. You can better analyze the situation and develop alternatives in terms of what needs to be done.

Learning Agility

This is something that we don't talk about very often, although we should. Learning agility is the ability to understand what needs to be done when you really have no clue. The chances are that you are proactive and you possess the ability to survive in difficult circumstances. If such is the case, the chances are that you are learning agile. If you already possess this trait, consider yourself lucky. If you don't, you can still cultivate it. Just step out of the comfort zone and try to expose yourself to unfamiliar situations. We human beings are natural problem-solvers. You might have some issues in the initial stages, but once you get more accustomed to your surroundings and the changing circumstances, you learn to adapt.

Influence

For most people, the word 'influence' isn't a good one, and it has been made that way with time. However, not many people take the time to realize that influence can only be bad if it is used to force people into something against their will. On the flip side, if you convince someone logically, you will get the desired outcome, but you will also create a bond with the other person - a bond based on trust. Suppose you can convince a group of people to do something or behave in a certain way. In that case, a time will come when you will be looked up to as an inspiring and charismatic leader. We need to understand that influence is the exact opposite of manipulation. Influence is something that includes transparency and authenticity. It also needs trust-building and emotional intelligence.

Respect

For a true leader, there is nothing more important than respect. He understands that only by giving respect can he gain it back. He tends to treat his team members and subordinates with respect and, therefore, end conflicts and tensions, giving birth to an environment where there are trust and confidence.

Courage

When it comes to voicing your opinion, coming up with a new idea, or providing feedback, the most important thing that a person needs is courage, which not many people have. However, one of the traits of a true leader is the fact that he is courageous and doesn't shy away from voicing his thoughts and feelings due to the fear of judgment or failure. He understands that if he keeps his mouth shut just to avoid a messy situation, he may have to clean up a bigger mess in the future. He chooses to fight a single fight on one day, rather than fighting a different fight each and every day.

Empathy

One of the qualities of effective leadership is empathy. Not only is it related to job performance, but it is also linked with emotional intelligence. If you are empathetic toward your subordinates, not only will you get the job done, but you will also become a likable figure in your superiors' eyes to whom you report. Empathy not only makes you more effective, but it also gives birth to a better work environment for those you command.

Compassion

A true leader is one who fears God above all else. Doing so, he cultivates in him the traits which bring him closer to God. One of those traits is compassion. A compassionate individual understands the issues and the problems of the people around him and his team. Compassion allows him to stay humble. Therefore, he gains the respect of the people around him. He is the one people look up to each time they are met with a difficult situation. This is the trait that was possessed by God's prophets. They were sent on this earth to spread kindness, love, and compassion. They were selfless individuals, and so is the person who leads through compassion.

Staying Motivated

No matter how strong or driven you are, you will always be met with certain roadblocks that are enough to shake your morale. When you are a leader, it happens more often than usual. The problem is that people look up to you for more motivation and encouragement. But all of us have a bad day when we don't feel like giving our 100% to the task at hand. That is exactly when we are in dire need of motivating ourselves.

"This is what the Lord says: 'Stand at the crossroads and look; ask for the ancient paths, ask where the good way is, and walk in it, and you will find rest for your souls."-Jeremiah 6:16

When you are a leader who is met with a tough situation, you need to step back, relax, take a deep breath, look at the situation, and analyze it. Often, we tend to make future decisions based on our past experiences, which isn't the right thing to do. You need to stay in the present and plan for the future, for you can't move forward if you are too preoccupied with what appears in the rearview mirror.

Staying Focused

One of the several things that differentiate between a leader and a follower is the focus. When you are out in pursuit of something great, you cannot rule out the possibility of obstructions, which are strong enough to shake your concentration and make you forget what you wanted to achieve in the first place. Take a look at the example of Moses, according to Exodus 15, which is as follows.

"They turned against Moses and complained. 'Why did you bring us here to die in the wilderness? Weren't there enough graves for us in Egypt? Why did you make us leave?' The people were enslaved for 430 years, and Moses freed them. They began to complain that "saying we're going to die in the wilderness" when they could have died as slaves. Furthermore, the conflict and complaints do not only come from the people but leaders as well. However, Moses stayed focus and he remembered what God said, "I will be with you."

A true leader doesn't let these challenges get in his way, nor does he lose focus in any way. When he is met with a hurdle, he reminds himself of the time when God told Moses, "I'll be with you."

Handling Criticism

Look around yourself. Every person on earth who has dared to think outside the box or do something differently from others has always been criticized initially. The difference is that a true leader believes that God is by his side and moves forward in the direction of his goals, and despite the initial setbacks, he doesn't scale down. Instead, he gets up bigger and better than ever. He knows that the criticisms that he faces mean nothing. All of his efforts are made in perfect accordance with the Lord's teachings, and those efforts are made for the betterment of the people. Here are a few ways in which the leader deals with criticisms.

- First of all, he doesn't play the victim. He is strong and shows it through the conviction, which is deeply embedded in his actions as well as the way he carries himself. Even if he is met with hardship, treachery, disease, and lack of resources, he continues to move forward and makes his rules along the way. He doesn't play the victim of the challenges, making it easier for him to focus on his goal and ways to accomplish them.

- Secondly, he doesn't take things too personally. He understands very well that all of his efforts are aimed toward the accomplishment of a bigger goal. Just in case a leader starts to take things personally, he gets distracted and takes his mind off the things that need to be done to accomplish his goals.

- Furthermore, a leader is a human being who doesn't like criticism. However, he holds his composure and doesn't let his emotions get the best of him. He doesn't react impulsively, for he knows that the slightest weakness on his part will go against him, his goal will be ruined forever, and the efforts he has made so far will all go in vain.

- Lastly, a leader knows very well how to turn criticism into an opportunity. No matter how many obstacles people put in his way through his words, he somehow dodges them all, and through the help from God, he maneuvers through. Then a time comes when he is applauded by the same people who once didn't believe in him, criticized him, and even made fun of him.

Discouragement for a Leader

As we have already discussed, a leader is also a human being. Even though he puts his firm faith in God, he also has emotions, and the sense of discouragement is one of them. Here are a few things that he has to go through that discourage and demotivate him, regardless of what a driven and spirited individual is.

Fear

Fear is a basic human impulse. It usually stems from inexperience. When you are out to do something or achieve something that you aren't too familiar with, fear kicks in. No matter how strong a person is, the fear of failure can eat up the glucose in his body. If the person allows the fear to seep in, it takes some time to overcome it. By the time he does, he has already missed out on some crucial opportunities, which can discourage him even further.

Failure

Let's suppose you have overcome your fear of failure and you continue to move forward with your goal. You put your best foot forth, and after some time, you end up in failure. All your efforts go to waste and you feel like winding it all up, not knowing that you might succeed the next time. Success doesn't come overnight. As a leader who believes in the divine necessity of what he is doing, basically, he needs to follow a trial-and-error approach. That is how the prophets of God have lived their entire lives. Their friends and families rejected these people, yet they stood firm, and that is the reason why they are loved and respected by numerous devotees all across the globe.

Frustration

Alright, so you didn't let fear seep in and you didn't even succumb to back-to-back failures. You hold on to the trial-and-error approach, hoping that you will succeed one day. However, you fail to realize that everything happens at the right time, only when God wants it to happen. And when you fail to realize this simple principle, you start doubting yourself. Due to repeated failures, you become frustrated, and that is exactly when you get discouraged. Life can be frustrating, but it shouldn't be frustrating enough to keep you from making a comeback, bigger, and better than ever.

Overcoming Obstacles: Some Quick Tips

We have already discussed that obstacles will continue to bother you as long as you are alive. If you are a leader, it will be much more difficult. Therefore, we have put together some quick tips to help you overcome obstacles in an effective manner.

- Define your priorities.
- Accept your fate, move on, and do not scale down your ambitions.
- Always keep the implications in mind. Zero in on the reasons for your disappointment as a problem-solver, rather than a person who likes to blame others for his failure.

- Despite the adversity, teach yourself to focus on the positives rather than the negatives.
- Talk less and listen more.
- Don't limit yourself and keep an open mind. You might end up with something valuable.
- Focus on the future, learn from the past, but stay in the present.
- Believe in your goal and lead from within.

Know that God is always by your side. There will be times when you will be abandoned, cheated on, and taken advantage of by your closest people, but they are mortal men with no real power. God possesses real power. He is the one who decides who should succeed and who shouldn't.

Chapter 7: Developing Your Style of Leadership

When you maintain an authoritative role, you often adopt a particular style needed to lead the people of your group. This is your approach to providing direction, implementing plans, and motivating your people. Most of the time, you develop your style based on your experiences and personality while keeping your organization's unique needs in mind. This style guides you in your role as a leader and allows you to recognize your strengths and weaknesses. Once this self-recognition sets in, you become more transparent in the messages you try to convey. It becomes easier for you to inspire the people around you and become better equipped to handle the challenges that come your way.

In a study conducted by Kurt Lewin in 1939, leadership styles were classified into three major groups*; autocratic, democratic,* and *laissez-fair.* His study formed the groundwork for proceeding theories. These three styles became the most broadly recognized among the many others that were born in the following years.

Autocratic

This style, also known as traditional, authoritarian, or command-and-control leadership, mainly emphasizes the distinction between the leader and its followers. In this approach, the leader issues command and makes key decisions without any input or consultation from the other team members. This type of leader is someone who is focused almost entirely on results and efficiency.

He expects others to do exactly what they ask them to do. They regard direct supervision as fundamental in maintaining a successful environment and followership. In this type of leadership, the reins are completely held by one person only who gives strict directives to their team members. It puts a single person in the position of utmost power.

You must only use this style in situations that require critical decisions to be made on the spot. You're the only one having the most knowledge on how to deal with it or when you're dealing with inexperienced new team members. There's no time to wait for them to gain familiarity with their role. However, the addictive properties of this type of control can sometimes lead to a misuse of power. It can overtake even the best leaders, making them more inflexible, intimidating, impatient, and unwilling to listen to other views. This feeling of superiority over others slowly manifests itself as arrogance, pride, and conflicts with the people being led.

"Power is what Pride really enjoys: there is nothing that makes a man feel so superior to others as being able to move them about like toy soldiers. It is spiritual cancer." ***-C. S. Lewis***

Many autocratic pastors justify their authority by saying that they were appointed by God Himself when that is really not the case. Rather, Christian leaders are directed not to be dictatorial or to lord it over others. Because power is not intended only to be a right but also a responsibility. If this kind of authority is practiced side by side with humility, the result can be quite prolific. This type of leader, having equal parts of compassion and commanding qualities, can easily get things done. Such a leader can have the ability to draw followers and present them with guidance down the right path. They can promote productivity through delegation and effective communication. Such a leader can lift other stresses by allowing their followers to be able to rely on them for important decisions.

Democratic

The democratic or participative style is considered to be the 'opposite' of autocratic leadership. In this style, the team members are considered and consulted before a decision is made. Although it is still the leader who makes the final call, every member has an equal say and every member's input is taken into consideration. The democratic style encompasses the notion that everyone should play a part in the group's decisions by virtue of their human status. A democratic leader always takes feedback from his team to ensure that every person is credited and their voice is heard. This style is primarily employed in places where innovative ideas are needed. Research suggests that this is the most effective way of leading, especially in places that require higher engagement. When many minds are at work, you develop better ideas and more creative solutions by looking at the different perspectives and the diversity of opinions.

"None of us is as smart as all of us." ***–Jean-Francois Cope***

Working under this type of leadership makes you feel empowered, valued, and unified while simultaneously increasing group morale. The leader is only there to give guidance and direction to the group's collective thoughts. While an autocratic leader might question disagreement as disloyalty, a democratic leader employs a more trusting and curious approach.

"If you want a system to heal, connect it more to itself."–The Servant Leader: From Hero to Host/ an Interview with Margaret Wheatley

A pastor can exercise this type of leadership by calling the group together to explore an important question, rather than having them stand in an expert position only to provide answers. This can encourage people to look for answers on their own when challenged with difficulties and decrease their dependency on others.

There are also a few downsides to this approach. It can't be applied everywhere, especially in situations where roles are unclear or time is essential, it takes a long time to organize big group discussions, obtain ideas and feedback, discuss possible outcomes, and communicate a decision. It can also add social pressure to members who don't like sharing their ideas in a group setting.

Laissez-faire

The French term *'laissez-faire'* roughly translates into *'let them do.'* This is the least intrusive form of leadership where the leader does not spend his time intensely managing his followers. Instead, he gives them all the rights and power to make decisions fully by themselves. It allows followers to self-rule while offering support and guidance when requested. The laissez-faire leader, using guided freedom, provides the followers with all the materials they need to accomplish their goals but does not directly participate in decision-making unless the followers request their assistance. This non-interference of the leader is sometimes important because it encourages accountability, creativity, and freedom of choice. It is also imperative that there is a proper delegation of tasks according to each member's capabilities. However, this style is only effective when the followers are highly skilled and experienced and when the followers can have a better knowledge of a particular situation than the leader.

Laissez-fair or delegative leadership is vital for the better functioning of the church. Some pastors are usually convinced that doing everything by themselves will ensure it is all well done. However, the church is like a living body. A single body part alone can do nothing unless all the other body parts work together. It was never God's design that the pastor would bear all the administrative responsibility; rather, God demonstrates several examples of delegation as a fruitful functionality among His people. The best example for us pastors is captured in the Book of Acts where we see the apostles build and establish the early church. Throughout the process, they were organizing, administrating, and delegating responsibilities to meet the needs of the establishment.

*"I invite everyone to choose forgiveness rather than division, teamwork over personal ambition." **–Patrick Lencioni***

Again, this style is not suited for use in every situation. It especially does not work for new members as they need guidance and hands-on support. Although this method empowers group members, it also sometimes limits their development and overlooks critical growth opportunities. This leads to a lack of structure, which can cause members to feel unsupported in their roles. This, in turn, may cause lower morale and an increased turnover rate.

Transactional

This type is considered an alias for authoritarian leadership by some, but it focuses more on performance. In this style, the leader imposes sanctions upon their followers to increase efficiency and establish routines and procedures. There are two factors that form the basis for this system: contingent reward and management-by-exception. The contingent reward provides materialistic or psychological rewards for good performance. Management-by-exception allows the leader to maintain the status quo. The leader intervenes when subordinates do not meet acceptable performance level and they initiate corrective action to improve performance. A transactional leader establishes standardized practices that help their members develop goal-setting, maturity, the efficiency of operation, and increased productivity. Transactional leaders facilitate the achievement of short-term goals through a clearly defined structure. However, not focusing on the organization's long-term goals can often cause adversity and stifle creativity.[1]

Transformational

Transformational leadership is where a leader works with teams to identify a needed change, creating a vision to guide through inspiration. This style focuses on clear communication, goal-setting,

---

[1] B. Becker (2020). The 8 Most Common Leadership Styles & How to Find Your Own. Hubspot. Retrieved from: https://blog.hubspot.com/marketing/leadership-styles

and motivation. A transformational leader is the type of person who is not limited by their followers' perception. His main objective is to work to change or *transform* their followers' vision and redirect their way of thinking. These types of leaders motivate their followers by becoming role models and enhancing the commitment, involvement, loyalty, and performance of followers. Transformational leaders have a stronger ability to adapt to different situations, self-manage, and be inspirational. They share a collective consciousness with their followers. This type of leader implements control by practicing idealized influence, intellectual stimulation, and individual consideration. Pastoral leaders need to bring about transformational change to individual members and congregations as a whole. Given the role of the overseer of a local church body, he must set an exceptional example for how his congregational members are to behave because those members will be looking to him to lead the way by both words and deeds *(Goodrich, 2013).*[2]

"Not many of you should become teachers, my brothers and sisters, for you know that we who teach will be judged with greater strictness." (James 3:1)

This is a highly encouraged form of leadership in growth-minded organizations because it motivates followers to see what they're capable of, but when dealing with a greater number of people, it isn't always effective because everyone could be at a different stage

---

[2] T. Gregory (2020). TRANSFORMATIONAL PASTORAL LEADERSHIP. Journal of Biblical Perspectives in Leadership. Retrieved from: https://www.regent.edu/acad/global/publications/jbpl/vol9no1/Vol9Iss1_JBPL_4_Gregory.pdf

of their learning curve. Some might miss out on the appropriate guidance because they are "too behind" or "too ahead."

Paternalization

Paternalism is defined as a system under which an authority undertakes to supply needs or regulate the conduct of those under its control in matters that affect them as individuals. A paternalistic leader acts as a parental figure, keeping his followers' best interests at heart. In return, he receives the complete trust and loyalty of their people. The relationship of the people with their leader is like a family. They can go to each other with any problem they have regarding their life. This creates more comfort and understanding between the leader and the people being led. People who follow paternalistic leadership also have better organizational skills and work harder to complete tasks to reach, or even exceed, their goals to please the parental leader.[3]

However, a shortcoming of paternalistic leadership is the possibility of bias between followers who maintained their loyalty and followers who were less loyal. This can inadvertently upset the hierarchal structure and cause unfair treatment.

Discover Your Leadership Style

When determining which style is right for you, you have to first keep a few things in mind.

[3] M. Rouse (2020). Paternalistic Leadership. TechTarget. Retrieved from: https://searchcio.techtarget.com/definition/paternalistic-leadership

- **Your position as a leader requires you to do:** Certain leadership styles are more impactful in specific roles. Each position requires a different set of habits to ensure the smooth running of your organization. You need to be self-aware of what your role is in the organization to be able to figure out which style suits you best.

- **A comprehensive list of all of your responsibilities:** You need to cater to specific situations with a specific mindset. It is crucial for you to know your responsibilities so you can develop traits accordingly to cater to those obligations.

- **What are your core values:** Your values affect the role you take as a leader. For instance, some people value paternal love in interaction with their followers, and thence, patriarchal or matriarchal leadership suits them better.

- **Would you rather make a decision on your own or collectively:** If you are more of an independent entity, it will suit you well to take on an authoritative role. Whereas, if you value a collective input more, it would be better for you to adopt a democratic style.

- **What does a healthy dynamic look like to you:** Another factor you need to consider is your growth notion. What you think is the best way to evolve as a group and what pushes you toward progress.

Leadership can be learned by actively seeking instruction on identifying, defining, and emulating the traits of effective leadership. It can also be learned by experimenting and trying out various approaches in different circumstances to see which result suits you best. Understanding your leadership style is the first step in developing your leadership skills. Once you recognize your style, you may well be on your way to becoming a great leader.[4]

[4] Indeed (2020). 10 Common Leadership Styles (Plus Ways to Develop Your Own). Retrieved from: https://www.indeed.com/career-advice/career-development/10-common-leadership-styles#2

Chapter 8: Cultivate Excellence

*"Whatever may be your task, work at it heartily (from the soul), as [something done] for the Lord and not for men." **(Colossians 3:23)***

Great leaderships are rare and qualities of excellence are hard to find, but as rare as they are, they aren't unattainable. Leaders are made when they accept their calling from God to lead but what separates a leader from becoming great is integrity, empathy, self-awareness, and the willingness to improve even further. To become one of the greats, we need to cultivate excellence within ourselves, train ourselves for our role, and always be ready to strive toward betterment.

"Leaders are made; they are not born. They are made by hard effort, which is the price that all of us must pay to achieve any goal that is worthwhile."

Vince Lombardi

God wants His people to abound in both inward and outward character and attain excellence in whatever we choose to do in this life. To do so, one must be open to new ideas and always be ready to adapt and improve. One must desire excellence in all life stages to make one's church, personal life, or organization advance to the next level. One must develop, learn, and use their prior knowledge to become better leaders. To do that, one must have a comprehensive understanding of themselves.

What people look for in a leader is not someone who merely points out the right and wrong. Instead, they look for someone who can *show* them what is right and what is wrong. People do not look for perfect leaders. They look for prepared leaders. Someone they can follow and someone who is willing to stand by their side and take them to the next level without any character judgment. Someone who helps them solve their problems and helps them stand on their own two feet. Someone who can prepare them for the challenges that are to come. A true leader may not necessarily have all the knowledge of this world, but they do have the wisdom that guides a man through all spheres of life. As Daniel's story goes, he was raised to the high office because of his wisdom and understanding.

"Then this Daniel was preferred above the presidents and princes, because an excellent spirit was in him; and the king thought to set him over the whole realm." **Daniel 6:3**

In Samuel 16, God was looking for a leader, a new king to rule over Israel, and He told Samuel He had chosen one of the eight sons of Jesse's family. Samuel thought the oldest would be chosen, but the Lord said to Samuel, *"Do not consider his appearance or his height, for I have rejected him. The Lord does not look at the things people look at. People look at the outward appearance, but the Lord looks at the heart."* These are the examples we should set before ourselves in our pursuit of excellence. While we strive to become better, we should do it for the glory of God. God chose David, the youngest son of Jesse, for He knew that David would be the most faithful, committed, and trustworthy in this job to lead the people.

Genuine spiritual growth and maturity come from seeking to do our best and knowing that what is best is part of God's will. However, there is a strict distinction between aiming for excellence and aiming for perfection. As finite human beings, none of us can attain the latter, for there is always room for growth in our endeavors. Excellence is a humble attempt at perfection, trying to strive for the better while keeping in mind that better does not mean faultless. Excellence must also not be treated as a quest for gaining superiority over others.[1] Only those who approach life looking for material or worldly gains treat the pursuit of excellence as a competition against others when it should only be a competition against their past self.

"Success means being the best. Excellence means being your best. Success, to many, means being better than everyone else. Excellence means being better tomorrow than you were yesterday. Success means exceeding the achievements of other people. Excellence means matching your practice with your potential."- Brian Harbour in Rising Above the Crowd

So you must not seek to excel simply to be better than others. You must let go of the spirit of competition and only struggle to attain the glory of God. Because the reality is that God sees our work and rewards us accordingly.

Communication

Another component of being a great leader is communication. You must know how to convey your message in a way that it becomes heard and understood by the masses. The leader can change the heart and mind of the one he leads, and to do that, they must know how to speak in a manner that would leave an imprint on others' minds. To do that effectively, the leader must first understand the *need* for that particular information to be heard. Why is it so important? How would it help others in their life? He needs to put himself in other's shoes and recognize the effect his message would have. The next thing he needs to do is to adopt his message so that different people from different communities having many different personalities can understand and be receptive to what he is trying to say.

As a leader, you will have to interact with many different kinds of individuals, so you need to know the most effective method of interacting with each other. This is essential for maintaining a healthy and productive relationship with the people you lead. Other than that, you must also be aware of your image in other people's eyes. People will only believe you if they know you are an honest person. People will only follow you if they know you carry wisdom to lead them to safety.

It is imperative for people to believe in you that you set yourself as a positive example, free from immorality and offense. It is also important to keep in check your body language and non-verbal cues because the words you choose make up only 7% of the message being conveyed. Things like the tone of your voice, hand gestures, and eye contact are key factors in ensuring engagement among interacting individuals. Perhaps the most vital part of communication is engagement.

You must know how to build and maintain a conversation, and for that, you need to master the art of listening. It is not only about sharing your thoughts, but it is also about taking their input. This would reinforce a two-way understanding between you and your followers. Not only that, but it would also allow your followers to understand each other, which would, in turn, build rapport and enhance their team efforts.

Team Building

When every individual in a group of people is using their skill set to the group's advantage, the group starts to make exceptional progress. This is because the individual talents and energies of the people combine to form a strong link. Collaboration brings along moral support. This motivation increases productivity in any situation.

The Bible has placed hard emphasis on teamwork. It says in Hebrews verse 10:25, *"Obtain spiritual growth and encourage one another."*

This is why we, as Christians, gather to worship together as one body of Christ. Corporate worship brings believers together as one family. It encourages personal and spiritual growth. It strengthens our bond as a community. According to Don Whitney in *Spiritual Disciplines*, "There's an element of worship that cannot be experienced in private worship or by watching worship. There are some graces and blessings that God gives only in the 'meeting together' with other believers." This community dynamic gives us a sense of belonging and fellowship.

Having consensus among the followers is, perhaps, the biggest asset for a leader, but to have that, a leader must know and understand his team building role. The leader is really the one who holds the team together and nurtures the collective effort. He guides the team members and motivates them to stay focused. His job is to help them develop skills according to their goals and objectives. He is the one who sets the direction to reach the said goals and objectives and he is the one who needs to resolve any kind of conflict as soon as it arises. To do all of this effectively, a leader must act as a mentor to the team members. He must teach them the importance of cooperation and the benefits of helping each other out. He must motivate them to perform even better by setting himself as an example.

Teaching people how to act with love and kindness toward one another allows us to become better in our faith and helps us become closer to God. As God says in the Bible,

"Let us think of ways to motivate one another to acts of love and good works." Hebrews 10:24-25

Chapter 9: Be a Follower before You Can Lead

At first glance, being a leader and being a follower seem like two completely different things. Being a leader means giving directions, having an impact, taking responsibility, directing and coordinating, and creating a drive in the people who follow you to lead them down the right road. While being a follower means to take directions, accept the impact, be dependent, walk in your leader's footprints, and go wherever they take you. Followership is often considered the antithesis of leadership when that is really not the case. Both of these notions aren't quite as different as you may think. There is a deep correspondence between becoming a leader and being a follower.

Like in any field, you must first be led before you start to lead. No successful leader is born with these qualities. He is taught to be following by being dependent on himself first. When a baby is born, they don't directly learn to walk and talk and do good things. Rather, they listen, observe, and learn by being dependent on their parents.

"He who cannot be a good follower cannot be a good leader." – ***Aristotle***

Leadership emerges as a consequence of the leader-follower dynamic. A person who wants to lead must first endeavor followership under the wing of a good leader. Only a leader who has been a follower first can understand the psychology and needs of the people they lead. That is how a leader learns self-discipline, integrity, and how to set a roadmap to success. These are the leaders who are actively engaged with their followers. These are the leaders who treat any task as a collective challenge rather than leaving it on the follower to complete. That is how a true leader is bred. He is bred in the footsteps of another great leader.

Such a leader is more responsive to his followers' demands and is open to learning new things. Thus, he is more liked by his followers and leaves a greater impact on their lives, which is what leadership is all about. It is about your social influence, not positional power. If you are a person in a leadership position and lack insight, motivation, and the ability to interact with others, then holding that position will do no good.

In the Bible, chapter Kings (12:1-24), when Rehoboam went to Shechem to become the King, the whole assembly of Israel approached him and said, "Your father put a heavy yoke on us, but now lighten the harsh labor and the heavy yoke he put on us, and we will serve you."

To this, Rehoboam told them to go away for three days and then come back to him, for that is when he would have an answer to their request. The King Rehoboam then consulted the elders who had served his father Solomon during his lifetime. He asked them, "How would you advise me to answer these people?"

These elders said to him, "If today you will be a servant to these people and serve them and guide them to a favorable answer, they will always be your servants."

King Rehoboam rejected their advice and went to the young men who had grown up with him and served him. He asked them what their advice was. They told him to be harsh toward the people instead of complying and heeding to their needs.

Hence, when the people came back after three days, the King said to them, "My father made your yoke heavy. I will make it even heavier. My father scourged you with whips. I will scourge you with scorpions." The King did not listen to the people, so the people rebelled against him until he fled.

"Rehoboam and the Law of Connection- Leaders touch a heart before they ask for a hand." ***(I Kings 12: 1-24)***

This event from the scripture is noteworthy because it teaches us that to be a great leader, you must be open to advice from your followers. You must learn from them and understand them. If you aren't on the same page with them, they will question your abilities and question your role and significance. If you cannot be open to their words, it will only breed resent and hate within their minds and they will not follow you. Instead, they will go against you, and you will be left with no followers. And what is a leader without any follower? So to understand how to be a good leader, you must first put yourself in the shoes of a follower and learn how to be led.

The Characteristics of a Good Follower

According to Robert Kelly, author of The Power of Followership, leadership only affects an organization's failure or success by 20%. The rest of 80% of the influence on an organization's effectiveness comes from the followers. So it isn't wrong to say that a follower's role plays a huge part in any organization.

To be a good follower, you must, first and foremost, be a good listener. You must be willing to take other people's advice. You must be willing to adapt whenever change is required. You must be respectful of your superiors and peers and remain mindful of what they want. You must have a deep understanding of everyone around you so you may thrive and flourish under their guidance, love, and support. You must be committed to what you do. You must constantly be trying to find new ways to follow directives. You must be competent enough to want to learn how to excel in whatever you do. If you ever think your leader is going down the wrong direction, you mustn't blatantly go against them.

But you must not be too afraid of advocating for the right thing. Although it may be risky sometimes to take a stand against your superiors and disagree with them, you must never be afraid to do it. You must always remember to do it in a respectful manner. You must be adept in the art of persuasion before you point out any flaw in their techniques.

This is where the birth of a leader lies. A true leader demonstrates the willingness to take a stand against any wrongs that they see. But to see a wrong, you must first know what is right. And to know what is right, you must carry wisdom within you, and if you do, you are potentially a natural leader. And you are capable of paving the way for other people to follow. So just how effective leadership is less about command and control and more about moral support and deliverables, effective followership is less about following instructions and more about a valuable contribution.

Chapter 10: Demonstrate Great

*"Greatness, generally speaking, is an unusual quantity of a usual quality grafted upon a common man." **-William Allen White***

Greatness is defined as the quality or state of being distinguished from the ordinary, i.e. having a higher degree of power, mental ability, or importance. It is the notion of being good at what you do and having the ability to leave an impact on the minds of others. Demonstrating greatness means to work to the best of your capabilities, take the initiative, and strive until you become a prominent and leading figure that people look up to. It means to show such quality in your work that has never been seen being done before to make things happen that were previously perceived to be unimaginable.

Historically, many people were deemed as one of the greats. From glorified warriors and military leaders like Alexander the third or Frederick the second to people who worked for humanitarian rights like Nelson Mandela and Mother Teresa. All of them had something in common. They did something that distinguished them from ordinary men. The world witnessed their relentless struggle to achieve their vision and it inspired them. It made them realize that one person can create a big change if he remains persistent.

To be an extraordinary leader, one must demonstrate this greatness and put best foot forward and first in every field. As Shakespeare once said, *"Be not afraid of greatness. Some are born great, some achieve greatness, and others have greatness thrust upon them."* Greatness lies within each and every one of us. We were all born with a unique set of traits distinguishing us from the rest, but what really determines whether you go on to become one of the greats is how you choose to demonstrate the qualities within you.

"The test of leadership is not to put greatness into humanity, but to elicit it, for the greatness is already there." --James Buchanan

So, greatness does not depend on your talents and virtues. It depends on how you choose to express them. To successfully demonstrate greatness, you must follow the following steps.

Desire to be Great

First and foremost, you need to have the desire to become someone who is revered, someone who is admired, or someone who has achieved great things within a short span of their lives. Desire can be a powerful driving force in all human beings, which can make any dream come true. It is the force that moves you to want to become better and great. It is the only thing that compels you to achieve success and makes you pursue your vision. It makes you want to do extraordinary things.

"The starting place for your greatness is desire. The desire to succeed, to serve others, to keep on going no matter what..." - Assegid Habtewold

Once you have the desire to be great, the motivation to do what needs to be done will follow suit. According to Joseph B. Wirthlin, *"Desire, burning desire, is basic to achieving anything beyond the ordinary."*

Have an Ambition

The next thing you need to do is to have a clear and set motive for what you want to achieve and a drive that makes you do it. You need to have a set mark or motive and you must be wholly and fully inclined to complete your motive and fulfill your purpose. Everybody in this world is sent with a purpose, which can be anything. Maybe you are destined to succeed in a particular field of sports or maybe you are destined to change the hearts of millions by your literary works. Maybe it is to become the CEO of the next best company or maybe it is to change the course of lives of the people around you. Your purpose could be anything that God has destined for you, but the caveat is to recognize that purpose and do something to accomplish the goal you have set. You must be ambitious and have a goal set out in front of you that you want to reach. You must have a dream that you want to fulfill.

"Never underestimate the power of dreams and the influence of the human spirit. We are all the same in this notion: The potential for greatness lives within each of us." -Wilma Rudolph

If you do not have a dream or a vision, you cannot possibly accomplish anything. There is always a set goal behind every success. Like Edmund Hillary said, *"People do not decide to become extraordinary. They decide to accomplish extraordinary things."*

Be Ready for Sacrifice

"You can only become great at that thing you're willing to sacrifice for." ***-Maya Angelou***

To achieve the goal that you set out to reach, you must be ready to do anything that is required to get there. You must be willing to make sacrifices and fight for attaining that position. You must be ready for all the struggles of this journey so you can transition from ordinary to one of the Greats. You must always be ready for an obstruction in your path to success and you must be mentally prepared on how you'll have to deal with it. You must not be procrastinating before starting an endeavor out of fear or laziness. You just have to get up and do it. In the wise words of John A. Passaro, *"There will never be 'the right time' in your life to do a great thing. You must create that time and greatness will follow."*

Be Creative

While struggling for success, you'll come across many roadblocks and challenges. To overcome these challenges, you must learn to think outside the box to find a solution that is most suitable for your situation. You must be creative enough to find ways out of and around a problem. An ingenious mind is essential for tackling difficult situations. In the words of Blaise Pascal, *"Man's greatness lies in his power of thought."* So, you must have that mental capacity to deal with issues along the way.

"If we are to be really great people, we must strive in good faith to play a great part in the world. We cannot avoid meeting great issues. All that we can determine for ourselves is whether we shall meet them well or ill." ***-Theodore Roosevelt***

Desire Service to Others

People like Martin Luther King Jr. and Mahatma Gandhi always pop up when we talk about people who did great humanitarian work. These were the people who demonstrated greatness by their service to humankind. These were the people who lived for something greater than themselves. They lived for the welfare of others and showed it by their selfless acts.

"When you live positively, it is impossible to not also be living for something greater than yourself." ***-Bryant McGill***

These people devoted their lives to others' service, which is why they became the greatest leaders of all time. So, in order for us to achieve greatness, we must put the greater good ahead of us and strive to make the lives of people around us better.

"Whoever renders service to many puts himself in line for greatness--great wealth, great return, great satisfaction, great reputation, and great joy." ***-Jim Rohn***

You must be kind and considerate toward whatever you choose to pursue. Even if it's something for your benefit, you must never do it at the cost of someone else's aspirations. If you are not kind, then what good is your success?

"Kindness is the essence of greatness and the fundamental characteristic of the noblest men and women I have known." ***-Joseph B. Wirthlin***

Build a Strong Character

The Greats, besides having an ambition and a drive to accomplish their goals, also have sound moral principles. Their virtues are such that they lead them to greatness. They have a well-established ethical code of conduct, which makes them firm in what they seek to accomplish.

"Sound moral principle is the only sure evidence of strength, the only firm foundation of greatness and perpetuity. Where this is lacking, no man's character is strong; no nation's life can be lasting." ***-Orson F. Whitney***

Therefore, we need to develop righteous values and be aware of our moral beliefs, for this awareness gives us a deeper sense of self and makes us undeterred.

Have an Influence

To demonstrate greatness, we must leave an impact on the minds of others. This is one of the most important things that allow you to become a great leader. According to Benjamin Disraeli, *"A great person is one who affects the mind of their generation."* To do this, you must not be afraid to share your knowledge, ideas, or concepts. You must be ready to show the world what you think and show them why it is important. You must be ready to lift others up with you and allow them to translate their knowledge. This cultivates respect for you in your followers' minds and allows you to have a lasting impression.

"You treat people with greatness, and greatness will come back to you." ***-Afrika Bambaataa***

Responsibility

To become a great leader is to take on a great responsibility. To be held accountable for not only your actions but also the actions of your followers. There are many great leaders in history who had to pay the price of imprisonment and execution for their followers' actions. This is why Winston Churchill once said, *"The price of greatness is responsibility."* This is the responsibility one must take in order to take a stand. You must take full responsibility for your actions, including making changes whenever you are criticized rather than getting offended.

*"The final proof of greatness lies in being able to endure criticism without resentment." **-Elbert Hubbard***

This is what it takes to become one of the Greats. Once you achieve this, you must not forget to be grateful that our Lord grants us success and makes our struggle not go in vain.

*"I know how to be brought low, and I know how to abound. In any and every circumstance, I have learned the secret of facing plenty and hunger, abundance and need. I can do all things through him who strengthens me." **–Philippians 4:12-13***

Chapter 11: How Great Leaders Inspire Others

"Leadership is about making others better as a result of your presence and making sure that impact lasts in your absence." – ***Sheryl Sanberg***

Perhaps the most important role you can play is of someone who inspires others to do better and be better. This role can make a big difference. It can allow you to impact others while simultaneously helping you reach your highest potential. According to Virgin Group Founder Sir Richard Branson, *the ability to inspire is the single most important leadership skill.* ***[1]***

Inspiration gives us a sense of meaning and a sense of purpose. It moves us out of the eternal void of procrastination and maneuvers us toward creating something meaningful out of our lives. It propels us to move forward. People consciously want to follow you when you inspire them. Imagine being that person who instills a belief into the hearts of others. Imagine having the ability to infuse energy and stir up the soul of another person. This is something all the great leaders have done. They had a vision and a direction that they knew would lead to a positive change. They gave purpose to the purposeless, gave them a drive, a passion, a commitment that made them change the course of their life.

Some leaders who left behind a great legacy and inspired millions of people:

Martin Luther King Jr.

Martin Luther King Jr. was a Baptist minister and a revered activist who led the Civil Rights Movement from 1955 until his death in 1968. In his early life, he saw his father, who was also a social rights activist, stand up against discrimination. Watching his father protest for voting rights and desegregation opened his eyes to the racial injustice faced by people of his kind. After the death of his father, he continued his work and became a member of the executive committee of the National Association for the Advancement of Colored People. In early December of 1955, he led the first great Negro nonviolent demonstration of contemporary times in the United States, the Montgomery Bus Boycott. For this, he was subjected to a lot of personal abuse but this didn't stop him. He went on to give speeches in two thousand five hundred different places and wrote five books and numerous articles. He directed a peaceful march in Washington where he delivered his famous address, "I Have a Dream."

The speech inspired the hearts of people all over America. On October 14, 1964, he won the Nobel Prize for combating racial inequality through nonviolent resistance. The impact of his efforts was so profound that they resulted in the passage of the Civil Rights Act of 1964 in desegregation of public accommodations. He was tragically assassinated in 1968, but he left behind a legacy that would change the lives of colored people around the globe. He became a national icon in the history of American liberalism and American progressivism.

Colin Powell

Colin Luther Powell was a military leader who, for over fifty years, devoted his life to public service. He held senior military and diplomatic positions across four presidential administrations. He became the first African-American Secretary of State in 2001. He was also the first and so far the only African American to serve on the Joint Chiefs of Staff. His parents were Jamaican immigrants. He grew up in Harlem and South Bronx sections of the New York City. He joined the army after graduating from college and slowly climbed his way up the political ladder. His view on freedom and his democratic values were highly admired by the masses. He went on to become a figure of African-American political progress. [1]

Steve Jobs

Steve Jobs co-founded Apple with his friend, Steve Wozniak, in 1997. He was a visionary who changed the future of computer technology. He revolutionized the world of communication by introducing the iPod, iPhone, and iPad. According to him, "The ones that are crazy enough to think that they can change the world, are the ones who do it." He believed innovation was what distinguished a leader from a follower. Under his leadership, the company thrived and developed numerous innovative products. His keen intuition and broad perspective led the company to success.

Barack Obama

Barack Hussein Obama was the 44th president of the United States and the first African American to serve in the office. His presidency lasted for two terms, in which he brought about extensive changes in policymaking. Although he didn't have much political experience, he had certain qualities that made him stand out. Some of these qualities were that he was an excellent orator. He effectively communicated with his people with a force that left an impact. He was culturally sensitive and placed immense importance on diversity and collective values. He had a positive mindset and a non-problematic attitude that made him reputable in the eyes of others. His influence only grew with his display of empathy and good-natured humor. He was able to set goals and make decisions that would pave the path to their fulfillment. He was an extraordinary leader and influencer.

Jesus

The greatest example of good leadership can be found in Jesus himself, our Lord and Savior. He submitted his life to sacrificial service under the will of God. He was a strong and extremely powerful leader, yet he also acted as a servant to his disciples. He wanted to set an example for his followers as a master as well as a servant. He emphasized the importance of selfless leadership when he chose voluntarily to go through Gethsemane and hang at the cross. He taught us there can be no real growth without freedom. He showed us that if we lead to control, then we are not leaders but selfish people. He said in Matthew Chapter 20, "Whoever desires to become great among you, let him be your servant. And whoever desires to be first among you, let him be your slave - just as the Son of Man did not come to be served, but to serve, and to give His life a ransom for many."

Jesus understood His people's problems and involved His followers in everything He did to enable growth and development in them. He was open and honest with His followers and focused on spreading love.

"As the Father has loved me, so have I loved you. Abide in my love." ***(John 15:9)***

Jesus believed in His followers and placed His trust in them. He did this not by taunting and having a strict demeanor but by believing in their potential. He taught us the importance of always striving toward becoming better, yet He never spoke ill of anyone's behavior. He was modest despite the immensity of His mission. His humility and humbleness are a great example for us. He says in Proverbs Chapter 16, *"Pride goes before destruction, and haughty spirit before a fall. Better to be of a humble spirit with the lowly than to divide the spoil with the proud."*

He encouraged and corrected His followers without any pride. His perseverance through difficult situations and wisdom made him admirable to His followers. Most of all, He held power and influence any leader must have. In an incident narrated in John Chapter 18, a mob approached Him seeking to take Him prisoner. He resolutely went forth 'Whom seek ye?' to which they replied Jesus of Nazareth and he said 'I am He.' As soon as he said this, they went backward and fell to the ground. He asked them again, and they gave the same reply, so He said, 'I have told you that I am he: if therefore ye seek me, let these (His followers) go their way.' His speech held confidence and He wasn't afraid of the consequences. If he were to give something, He would give it His all.

After studying these people, we realize it wasn't their ideas that distinguished them from other people. It was their ability to inspire a change. So if we want to become eminently successful, we must inhabit these qualities within and strive relentlessly toward our goal. We must always remember to have faith in the midst of it all, for God gives us power and the ability to move toward success.

Great Leadership and Problems of the Contemporary Society

Great leadership is a fundamental prerequisite for the well-being of any social institution. Especially in today's modern society with its many present-day challenges, great leadership is required to hold people together and provide a sense of moral relief, justice, and relative stability to counter this chaotic world. The church can play an important role in this part. With the aftermath of Trump's presidency leaving America in distraught, inciting violence among his followers, and making unjust policies, someone needs to take a stand to bring this country back together, and great pastoral leadership can allow us to improve our ways and help us work as one. By promoting healing, equality, and social justice, pastoral leaders can bring a sense of community and help us improve our ways.

"But avoid foolish and ignorant disputes, knowing that they generate strife. And a servant of the Lord must not quarrel but be gentle to all, able to teach, patient, in humility correcting those who are in opposition, if God perhaps will grant them repentance, so that they may know the truth, and that they may come to their senses and escape the snare of the devil, having been taken captive by him to do his will." (2 Timothy 2:23-26)

The church plays an important role in providing moral principles that guide many Christians' everyday lives while also serving as a guide for political and economic policymaking. The catholic social teachings are a component of the moral order. If the church has access to excellent leaders who have keen insight and profound wisdom, it can leave an enormous impact on the workings of our society. This way, we can restore love, peace, and harmony in people's lives and work toward growth and betterment. Some contemporary problems that the church can help solve are:

Unjust Policies

*"Woe to those who make unjust laws, to those who issue oppressive decrees, to deprive the poor of their rights and withhold justice from the oppressed of my people, making widows their prey and robbing the fatherless. What will you do on the day of reckoning, when disaster comes from afar? To whom will you run for help? Where will you leave your riches? Nothing will remain but to cringe among the captives or fall among the slain." **(Isiah 10:2-4)***

Although the church does not hold the position to make political statements, it can still set a moral standard for policies and speak up against the unjust ones. Pastors can raise awareness during church gatherings and congregations on what ethics a person should keep in mind while making any decision, especially when making a decision that affects the masses. If the church fails to speak up against immoral social policies, or even worse, supports them, it becomes complicit. This has happened before when some churches in the U.S. opposed civil rights for African Americans. The church knows what is permissible and what is morally impermissible as it has been clearly written in God's word, which is why it is its duty to speak up when they see people, or a group of people, being wronged.

*"Do your best to present yourself to God as one approved, a worker who has no need to be ashamed, rightly handling the word of truth." **(2 Timothy 2:15)***

Due to Trump's anti-immigration policies, many immigrants have suffered. In cases like these, the church must be ready to give humanitarian aid to migrants and educate people about the downsides of such a policy. The church should remind them about God's blessings on the one who is generous and offers help to the one who needs it.

*"But if anyone has the world's goods and sees his brother in need, yet closes his heart against him, how does God's love abide in him?" **(1 John 3:17)***

Poverty

With our Nation's poverty rate rising at the fastest pace in history, someone needs to be there to bridge the gap between the rich and the poor. Local church involvement can allow the poor to lead a better life. The church can raise money to develop housing and food distribution programs. God has said in Proverbs 22:9, "Whoever has a bountiful eye will be blessed, for he shares his bread with the poor."

The church can also bring the rich and poor together during congregation so that they may share each other's suffering. This can improve their attitude toward one another by generating a feeling of love, which can cause them to offer help. Pastors can even deliver sermons that can raise their altruistic sense and make them more charitable.

"For there will never cease to be poor in the land. Therefore, I command you, 'You shall open wide your hand to your brother, to the needy and to the poor, in your land." ***(Deuteronomy 15:11)***

Racism

Racism is one of the major issues in American culture. It is, sadly, still prevalent in our society despite many efforts to remove it. The church deals with a diversity of the population. It must not be a place of ethnic and social divisions if it were to thrive. The church should not wander around the sidelines when it comes to this social dilemma; rather, it should make leading efforts for racial reconciliation.

"Open your mouth for the mute, for the rights of all who are destitute. Open your mouth, judge righteously, defend the rights of the poor and needy." ***(Proverbs 31:8-9)***

"And he made from one man every nation of mankind to live on all the face of the earth, having determined allotted periods and the boundaries of their dwelling place." ***(Acts 17:26)***

The church is designated to ensure equality among God's people and should treat it as its first and foremost mission. Christians, especially, should not subject each other to discrimination for their appearance as God shows no partiality between His people (Romans 2:11). Church pastors should explicitly deliver sermons relaying God's message of equality. During congregation, they should ensure solidarity and collaboration between people of different ethnicities. Mutual understanding and acceptance among ethnic groups is an imperative part of this religion. It is the only way we can obtain genuine solution to our contemporary problems.

Misogyny

With feminism on the rise, we see, every day, how women had been oppressed for years and are still subjugated due to social and cultural expectations and bias. Even in today's age, it is hard for them to demonstrate their true potential. God created both men and women equal. He says in Galatians 3:28, "There is neither Jew nor Greek, there is neither slave nor free, there is no male and female, for you are all one in Christ Jesus."

It is the church's duty to take a stand for women who are being oppressed as women are an integral part of our society. They were created in God's image just like men (Genesis 1:27) and have made as many contributions in this world.

Solving these contemporary problems is not only the church's responsibility, but it is also every leader's responsibility. Entrepreneurs and CEOs should adopt and maintain policies that protect people who are oppressed and prevent discrimination. They should make their work environment appropriate for all kinds of people. They should not show any discrimination between people of color and those from different ethnicities. Neither should they have unfair pay gaps between people of different genders. They must ensure there is equality in all that the company seeks. Once they do that, their corporation will flourish.

Chapter 12: Believe in Yourself

Before one takes on any task, one must believe that they fit the role. A man can have a remarkable skill set and extraordinary abilities, yet if he doesn't believe in himself, all of those can go down the drain. Courage, consistency, and conviction are the three things that can lead any man to success, even if the man isn't of exceptional stature. A man having courage isn't afraid of the obstacles he might come across while pursuing his dreams.

He is ready to face any challenge head-on. Having consistency will make sure he doesn't slack off and that he keeps pushing forward at a steady pace. Finally, having a conviction will make sure he never gives up. When a man has this belief that his dream is of value, his skills are of value, or he is of value, he can go to great lengths to do what needs to be done in order to accomplish his goal. This is the tenet that pulls you through every failure and every struggle so that you may try again. When a heart is full of conviction, no amount of judgment or speculation can deviate you from your path.

How you view yourself and measure your value are two keen aspects of self-belief and success. Even if a tiny amount of doubt exists within you, it can create a barrier between you and your goal. It is very important that you deem yourself worthy before anyone else follows in your footsteps because if you don't believe in yourself, no one else will. If you do not believe you are worthy of being followed, why on earth would anyone follow you? If you don't have faith in your product, how would you convince investors to finance it? If you don't trust your decisions, why would someone else?

Roy T. Bennet said in his book, *The Light in the Heart,* "Believe in your infinite potential. Your only limitations are those you set upon yourself. Believe in yourself, your abilities, and your potential. Never let self-doubt hold you captive. You are worthy of all that you dream of and hope for."

So recognize your gifts, lead with confidence and optimism, and do the things you would do if there was no room for failure, except being open to failure. Take failure as an opportunity to improve. Have faith in yourself and be grateful for the abundance around you. Because as a leader, you will need to have the potential always to pull through. No matter what happens, no matter how many setbacks you might have to face, it is your duty as a leader to stay on course.

Even if the world tells you that this is something not meant for you or that you are out of your mind for believing this could work, you must always stick to your strategy. You must always have enough faith in your potential not to be deterred by whatever others might say. We are continuously conditioned to doubt ourselves by words like these. Although this doubt prevents us from making unfavorable decisions, too much of it can hinder us from our goal. We must lead with hindsight and intellect, and once we take a step forward, we must continue down the same track. We must always continue to move forward.

Prime your mind with thinking that there is no margin for backing out. Once your mind acknowledges this, you will be able to reach unprecedented levels of prosperity.

"You may be the only person left who believes in you, but it's enough. It takes just one star to pierce a universe of darkness. Never give up." – ***Richelle E. Goodrich, Smile Anyway: Quotes, Verse, and Grumblings for Every Day of the Year***

How to Enable This Belief

To have firm conviction and self-reliance, you must edify your mind through positive affirmations. You must remind yourself of your worth and know that you have God's aide by your side. Trust that you need nothing more. Although this can seem like a bizarre idea, talking to yourself and reminding yourself of how great and absolutely unique you are can profoundly affect how you carry yourself through this world. Now this is not something that is *rumored* to have a positive impact on your identity. There are neuroscience and psychology that back up this claim. One such theory is *the self-affirmation theory* proposed by Steele in 1988. It is made around the idea that we can maintain our sense of self-integrity by affirming what we believe in positive ways. This self-integrity affects our global self-efficacy, which is our perceived ability to control moral outcomes and respond flexibly when our concept of self is threatened (Cohen and Sherman, 2014). However, maintaining a self-identity is not only about being extraordinary but also about being competent and adequate in areas that we personally value. This theory has been proven by conducting MRI scans in a number of people and it has come to pass that what you think about yourself affects how you process information and how you relay it forward.

Throughout our lives, we make innumerable amount of blunders and mistakes with only a handful of times where we are actually successful. To counter doubts and negative thoughts, we need to preserve our self-worth in the face of these shortcomings. All we need do is talk to ourselves every morning and say, *"You are awesome."* Tell yourself that you are great and you can do extraordinary things and that failure is only a chance to improve, so the more you fail, the better you will become. This not only elevates your sense of self but also minimizes stress, anxiety, and negative ruminations, enhancing your overall mental health.

Another tool you can use to create a stronger mindset and get in better touch with yourself is meditation. Meditation is a practice where an individual uses techniques such as mindfulness, focus, and mental awareness to reach a clear, emotionally calm, and stable state. It is a discourse of expression and a journey that leads you to a deeper understanding of things. By making meditation an everyday practice, you can achieve higher levels of self-esteem and self-awareness. While meditating, you ruminate on your reality and come to many realizations that help you break through. You grow in confidence while simultaneously reducing your stress and anxiety. It helps foster kindness and allows you to find your inner self. It improves your physical and mental health and enables a higher level of learning. Meditating regularly prevents burnout and ameliorates your strength and happiness.

Self-reflection is an important part of our everyday life. If we reflect on ourselves with doubt and uncertainty, we are doomed never to attain followership. If we regard ourselves with negative opinions, others will do the same because how you view yourself makes up a great part of how others view you. Only if you make peace with your thoughts, fight those doubts, and welcome the uncertainty would you be destined for good.